JOSHUA'S LONG DAY AND JONAH'S LONG NIGHT: FACTS OR FAIRY TALES?

Volume XII
Creation Science Series

by Dennis G. Lindsay

Published by
Christ For The Nations Inc.
P.O. Box 769000
Dallas, Texas 75376-9000

Printed 1997
© 1997

All Scripture NIV unless otherwise noted.

ACKNOWLEDGMENTS

A number of organizations have aided my research in preparing and producing this book. To them I wish to express special appreciation and acknowledgment.

The Creation Life Publishers of San Diego, California; *Creation Ex Nihilo* magazine of Australia; Bible-Science Association of Minneapolis, Minnesota; Institute For Creation Research of El Cajon, California; The Genesis Institute of Richfield, Minnesota; Creation Evidences Museum of Glen Rose, Texas and Films for Christ of Mesa, Arizona.

These organizations have been evangelical Christianity's foremost defenders of Creation Science. For their substantial contribution to my own life and ministry, I personally wish to thank them and their staffs. I highly recommend their materials to those who wish to keep abreast of the events in the ongoing struggle between the forces of light and darkness regarding the creation-evolution issue.

AUTHOR'S NOTE

To receive the full impact and significance of the message of this volume, it is strongly recommended that Volume VI of the Creation Science Series titled *The Original Star Wars and the Age of Ice* be read prior to reading this volume. It lays a foundation for understanding many Bible passages pertaining to the judgment of evil nations. These judgments are associated with cataclysmic events which originated in the physical heavens. Volume VI examines astral-related catastrophes which have occurred throughout mankind's history and are documented both by the ancients' records as well as in the Earth's geology. Creation Science and the Bible both concur with these evidences of catastrophism.

This volume, *Joshua's Long Day and Jonah's Long Night: Facts or Fairy Tales?* is a powerful witness for the validity of Scripture in general and the incredible miracle stories of Joshua and Jonah.

FOREWORD

The purpose of the Creation Science Series is simply to make information available to all laypersons interested in the subject. My intent is to provide support for Creation Science that is easy to read and comprehend, while leaving out much of the technical jargon that only a specialist would appreciate. Those who desire additional information and documentation by experts in the Creation Science community may contact the following outstanding organizations:

MASTER BOOKS
    9260 Isaac St., Suite E
    Santee, CA 92071

INSTITUTE FOR CREATION RESEARCH
    2100 Greenfield Dr.
    Box 2667
    El Cajon, CA 92021 USA

BIBLE-SCIENCE ASSOCIATION
    P.O. Box 33220
    Minneapolis, MN 55422-0220

CREATION EVIDENCES MUSEUM
    Box 309
    Glen Rose, TX 76043

GENESIS INSTITUTE
    7232 Morgan Ave S.
    Richfield, MN 55423

APOLOGETICS PRESS INC.
    230 Landmark Dr
    Montgomery, AL 36117-2752

Cover design by Don Day and illustrations by Camille Barnes.

TABLE OF CONTENTS

Introduction 13

**PART I: BUILDING A CASE FOR JOSHUA
            AND JONAH'S CREDIBILITY**

    **SECTION I: MISCONCEPTIONS
                            ABOUT THE BIBLE**

1 Who is Hindering Scientific Progress? 21
2 The Bible Was First 32
3 Atheism Comes Full Circle and
    Attacks Its Own 38
4 The Ends, Corners and Pillars of a
    Flat Earth 44
5 The Sunflower Takes First Place;
    the Sun, a Close Second 52

    **SECTION II: HOT ISSUES ABOUT GOD
                            AND HIS WORD**

6 Why Did God Do It? 67
7 Is God a God of War? 69
8 Another Holocaust? 71
9 The Moral Governor of the Universe 74
10 The Moral Depravity Was Beyond
     Description 79
11 Bringing It Closer to Home 85
12 God's Ultimate Objective 89
13 What About the Women and Children? 92
14 Ample Warning 95
15 The Key to Lasting Greatness 98
16 Time for Housecleaning 108

17 Why Was Israel Chosen as an
    Instrument of Judgment? 112
18 God is Humane 117

PART II: JOSHUA'S LONG DAY

SECTION III: HOW DID GOD DO IT?

19 Supernaturalistic 122
20 Plotting the Course 128
21 Clue One: Tilt, Tilt, Tilt 133
22 Clue Two: Ancient Lava Flows and
    Flying Magnetic Saucers 140
23 Clue Three: Earth's Heavenly Attraction .. 146
24 Clue Four: The Day the Compass Dies ... 152
25 Clue Five: Heavenly Beach Ball Buddies .. 157
26 Just for Fun 165

**SECTION IV: LOOK UP FOR YOUR
               JUDGMENT DRAWETH
               NIGH**

27 Hot Rock From Heaven 172
28 "Floodgates of the Heavens"
    (Heavenly Fallout) 178
29 The Formation of Meteorites 181
30 Exploding Heavenly Bombs and
    Other Biblical Catastrophes From Above ... 192

SECTION V: HISTORICAL EVIDENCE

31 Additional Ancient Documentation 202
32 Who Moved the Sun? 210
33 The Day the Sun Wandered Crazily
    Across the Sky 220
34 "The Earth Reels Like a Drunkard" 224

35 The Mysterious Retrogression of the
   Shadow 236
36 The Greatest Miracle of Joshua 10 242
37 Postscript Warning 247

PART III: JONAH'S LONG NIGHT

SECTION VI: A WHALE OF A TALE

38 Darts of Doubt 253
39 Sounds a Little Fishy to Some 256
40 Jonah II 263
41 Here Am I, Lord, Send Someone Else 268
42 The Jonah Principle: How to Miss
   God's Boat 277
43 The Alien From the Sea:
   Jonah and the Fish God 281
44 The Proof of Jonah's Authenticity 288
45 The Greatest Miracle of Jonah 295
46 Postscript: One More Lesson for Jonah . . . 298

PART IV: THE PROPHETIC SIGNIFICANCE
OF JOSHUA AND JONAH

SECTION VII: THE GODS OF
CATACLYSM

47 Ancient Mythology and
   Astral Catastrophism 302
48 Worldviews of the Ancients 307
49 The Origins of Astrology 311
50 The Abominations of the Pagans 320
51 The Gods of the Greeks 323
52 The Gods on Our Calendars 333
53 Halloween and Friday the 13th 337

54 Cosmic Warfare and Hairy Comets 339
55 What if We Had Been Alive in
     Those Days? 350
    **SECTION VIII: THE COMING
              HOLOCAUST**

56 The Doomsday Asteroid 355
57 A Foretaste of the Final Judgment 361
58 Consider the Ominous Words of Jesus 364
59 Revelation and the Coming Judgment 370
Conclusion: You be the Judge 383
Endnotes 387
Bibliography 392
Illustrations 396

Figure #1. THE MISSING DAY

Introduction

Did the U.S. Space Program Find a Missing Day?

Space scientists at Greenbelt, Maryland were checking out the positions of the sun, moon and planets in space to calculate where they would be positioned in 100 years and in 1,000 years. This information is vital in sending satellites to designated places. As computer calculations were made backward and forward over the centuries of time, the results continually manifested a discrepancy. Troubleshooters were called in to check out the computer system, but the problem persisted: A day was missing in space in elapsed time. Computer calculations continually yielded dates of certain historical astronomical events such as eclipses and the arrangement of planets to be a day later or slightly different in arrangement than what historical manuscripts recorded.

For example, ancient astronomers recorded a full eclipse of the sun on a specified date. However, according to the information fed into the computers as to where the sun, moon and Earth are at present, the eclipse should have taken place, not on the date which the ancient astronomers recorded, but on the previous day. A day was found missing. The only possible explanation was found in Joshua 10:13, when the "sun stood still" and the daylight was extended. Sounds pretty amazing, right?

The Truth of the Matter.

No doubt most everyone has heard or read this account or at least a similar report. Is it true? Well, there may be some truth to it; however, there is more to it than what the average Christian tract usually prints. In fact, some have denied its validity entirely, suggesting that it was concocted by some overly zealous Christians.

The account of the Long Day found in Joshua 10 is one of the most remarkable records in the Bible. It seems impossible and therefore unbelievable. Yet this incredible account is recorded as having taken place during Israel's conquest of the Promised Land. Every triumph of the Israelites recorded in the Bible passages preceding and following this one has been confirmed and documented in recent years by archaeological discoveries.

One prominent scholar and archaeologist, Dr.

Nelson Glueck, president of the Hebrew Union College, stated, "As a matter of fact, it may state categorically that no archaeological discovery has ever controverted (*invalidated* or *discredited*) a biblical reference. Scores of archaeological findings have been made which confirm in clear outline or exact detail historical statements in the Bible." [1]

Fairy Tale, Myth or Allegory?

Is the biblical account of Joshua's Long Day a fairy tale, a fable or a myth? Or is it an allegory containing good moral and ethical principles to build character, yet did not actually occur in history? Is the biblical story of Jonah being swallowed by a great fish an ancient whale of a tale? How could Jonah possibly survive three days and nights in the belly of a whale?

Both of these biblical accounts will be explored in this volume. We will not only observe the amazing truth of these stories, but we will also grasp the spiritual significance of each message, which God desires His children to fully understand.

The Issues and What is at Stake.

In Part II of this volume, we will consider such questions regarding Joshua 10 as:

1. What is the greatest miracle of the passage?
2. Why did God do it?
3. How did God do it?
4. What other historical records besides the Bible disclose information about the event?

There are several other hot issues involving God's character that need to be explored. Is the God of the Bible a God of war? How can He be a God of love and command the Israelites to exterminate the people of the Promised Land, including women, children and animals.

In Part I, we will take a look at a prominent challenge against God's Word, which some believe is one of the chief hindrances to the progress of science. Christians have taught that the Bible is infallible and without error. Skeptics claim that passages like Joshua's Long Day and the story of Jonah have been used to confuse children and adults into believing impossible events that never could have happened.

Let us take up the challenge and see if it is the Church that is responsible for the hindrance to the progress of science or if it is the atheistic evolutionary humanists who are actually the ones responsible for blocking the advancement of science and the enrichment of life.

In Part III of this volume, we will explore the story of Jonah. What are the scientific difficulties which are found within the book of Jonah? Have any accounts of a similar event been recorded in modern times? Why didn't Jonah want to go to Nineveh? What kind of creature could actually swallow a human? What was the greatest miracle of the book?

In Part IV, we'll study the ancient gods to answer such questions as: Why did man become so interested in planetary worship after the Flood? Why was there so much cosmic warfare in ancient mythology? Why were the ancients dedicated to the construction of temples related to astronomical phenomena? Did you know that the days of the week and some of the months of the year are named after the sun, moon and planets? Why has Friday the 13th become a symbol of an unlucky day? What is the origin of Halloween, and why is it still celebrated by many?

Finally, we will examine the prophetic significance of Joshua and Jonah — how their accounts relate to future events predicted in Scripture that point to judgment on Earth coming from the heavens. We will look at scientific discoveries that confirm predictions made by Christ and outlined in the book of Revelation.

PART I
BUILDING A CASE FOR JOSHUA AND JONAH'S CREDIBILITY

SECTION I
MISCONCEPTIONS ABOUT THE BIBLE

Chapter 1:   Who is Hindering Scientific Progress?

Chapter 2:   The Bible Was First

Chapter 3:   Atheism Comes Full Circle and Attacks Its Own

Chapter 4:   The Ends, Corners and Pillars of a Flat Earth

Chapter 5:   The Sunflower Takes First Place; the Sun, a Close Second

Figure #2A. SCIENCE VERSUS RELIGION

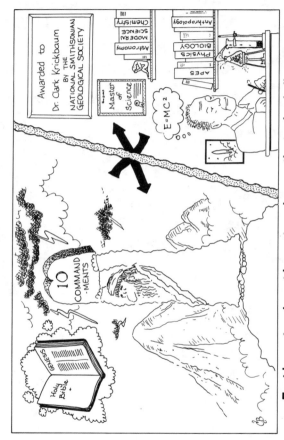

East is east and west is west; and never the twain shall meet.

Chapter One

Who is Hindering Scientific Progress?

Figure #2B. SCIENCE VERSUS RELIGION

Attacks by Skeptics.

> Its (the sun's) rising is from one end of
> the heavens, and its circuit to the other
> end of them; and there is nothing
> hidden from its heat (Psa. 19:6 NAS).

This passage has amused Bible critics in the
past, for they claimed the writer of this verse
believed the unscientific notion that the sun
revolved about the Earth. If the Earth really did
revolve around the sun, it was reasoned that the
inhabitants of Earth would be bombarded with a
constant violent wind. Therefore, they
concluded that the Earth could not be moving.

This passage and the passage describing
Joshua's command for the "sun to stand still"
have been used to criticize the Church's view that
the Bible is without error. The Church has been
blamed for the absurd belief during the Dark
Ages that the Earth is the center of the solar
system, and the sun, moon and planets revolve
around it. Actually, God's Word confirms just the
opposite, but the Church failed to realize this
back in the Dark Ages.

Scientists Excommunicated From the Church.

As a result of their misconceptions, the
Church fathers excommunicated a couple of

God-fearing scientists. Clergyman and Polish astronomer Copernicus and Italian astronomer and physicist Galileo disagreed with the Church's belief that the Earth was the center of our solar system. In the 1500s, Copernicus and in the 1600s, Galileo, with his newly invented telescope, made all kinds of discoveries. They began to convince people that the Earth really did move and that the sun is the center of our planetary system.

Their discovery that day and night result from the Earth turning on its axis, not from the sun traveling around it, challenged the traditional views of the Church fathers. Even Martin Luther was severely disturbed by the theories of Copernicus. So Galileo and Copernicus were excommunicated because they refused to renounce their views. Not until a few years ago did the Catholic church put them back into good standing.

The world laughs at such resolutions and mocks the Church, inferring that science has been held up by ridiculous beliefs. Although the Church is not beyond making mistakes, it is actually Christianity that leads to the progress of science. Wherever the Bible is freely read and obeyed, the door is open for the advancement of science.

It was the Reformation that led to an

explosion of science. Up until that time, the Bible was not available to the common people. But as it was translated from Latin into various languages and freely read, a spiritual revival spread throughout Europe. Man came in touch with his Creator, and this led to the advancement of science.

Skeptics to Blame.

It was not the Church that came up with the concept of the Earth being the center of the solar system. This idea was actually concocted in about 130 by Ptolemy, a Greek geographer and astronomer of Alexandria. Ptolemy taught this view, and for centuries people accepted his idea that the Earth stands still and is at the center of the universe. **(See fig. #3.)**

Ptolemy was neither a Jew nor a Christian. His dogma was not based on biblical teaching nor upon evidence. But because he was highly educated, the scientific community accepted his theory as fact. His theory became widely accepted. When pressure was eventually put on the Church to accept this theory, theologians began looking for Scriptures to confirm this view. The passage containing Joshua's account of the Long Day was believed to substantiate Ptolemy's false concept, and the Church adopted

Figure #3. A PAGAN CONCEPTION

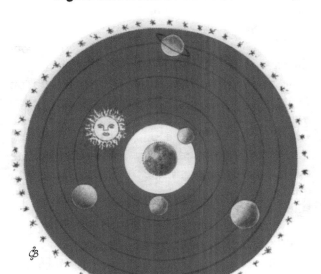

this pagan idea.

20th Century Repeat.

Today, we have a similar situation. Some Christian scholars have attempted to combine the biblical account of creation and the atheistic myth of evolution. They rationalize that since evolutionists have "proven" the Earth is 4.6 billion years old and the various layers of the Earth appear to have taken hundreds of millions of years to form, God's Word must have passages which confirm an ancient Earth.

Once a person realizes that the basic issue with the evolutionist is not the "evidences" but the existence of God, he can see that the immense ages assigned to the Earth are not based on evidence, but theory. For the atheist, the theory *must* be true, because the only alternative is the Christian view of a special creation by God.[2]

There is no need to try and accommodate evolutionism by attempting to harmonize it with the biblical account of creation. The Bible can stand on its own.

Joshua's Command Was Correct.

Actually, it is unscientific to criticize Joshua's command for the sun to stand still, or to find fault with anyone who makes such a statement, because all motion is relative. This means that no one knows where in the universe there may be a fixed point with zero motion.

From man's viewpoint on Earth, the sun rises in the morning, moves across the sky, and sets in the evening. This is why even scientists still use words and phrases that some do not consider to be scientifically accurate.

Yet the whole science of nautical and engineering astronomy is based on an assumption made purely for convenience sake: The Earth is in the center of a great celestial sphere in which the sun, moon, planets and stars are in their appointed and ordered paths. This is for practical use, so that positions of the planets can be determined and scores of other applications made in order to send probes into space to explore our solar system.

The Orbit of the Sun.

As a matter of fact, neither the sun nor any other point in the universe is motionless — from a scientific standpoint. **(See fig. #4.)** Scientific textbooks reveal that our sun, along with its entire solar system, revolves around the center of its own galaxy at the tremendous speed of 481,000 miles per hour. This gigantic orbit would require over 200 million years to complete.

At the speed of 64,000 mph, our sun is carrying all its planets through space toward the star cluster known as Hercules, which is on the edge of our galaxy, the Milky Way. And our galaxy is moving around the center of a supercluster of 2,500 other galaxies at 1,150,000 mph.

The Earth's motion, relative to the universe, has been measured at 360,000 mph. How scientists determine the velocity of the various celestial movements is something few can fully

Figure #4. THE DANCE OF THE UNIVERSE

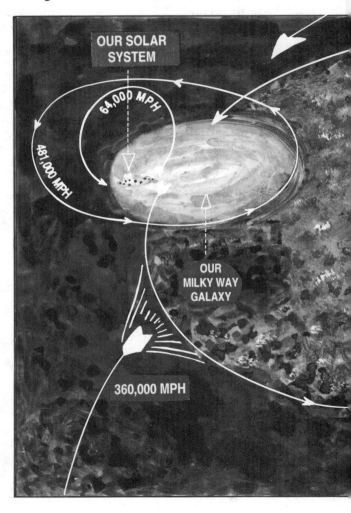

CLUSTER OF 2,500
NEIGHBORING
GALAXIES

1,350,000 MPH

UNIVERSE

understand and appreciate. But the truth is, God has created a dynamic universe that is in constant rotating motion as if it were one beautiful galactic choreographical dance.

One purpose of the circular motion of all objects in space is to provide stability. If planets and moons did not have orbital motion, the force of gravity would cause them to crash inward. If the stars in the Milky Way were stationary, they would begin moving toward the center and collapse within the galaxy. The galaxy's rotation prevents this, maintaining stability throughout the universe.

The easiest way to measure the movements of heavenly bodies is to assume a fixed point; in ancient times and in modern times, the Earth has been chosen as this fixed point. That is because it is most convenient for man to consider the Earth as a fixed point with the sun moving around it. So even Joshua's choice of words, "sun, stand still" (Josh. 10:12), in this context is perfectly modern and correct. And the sun's circuit is from one end of the heavens to the other, just as Scripture states.

Earth's Major Motions.

The following is a partial list of Earth's separate motions in space:

Motion	Speed
1. Rotation of Earth	1,000 mph at equator
2. Earth's orbit around sun	66,600 mph
3. Solar system circular travel around star cluster within our galaxy	64,000 mph
4. Solar system circular travel around the galaxy	481,000 mph
5. Overall circular motion of the galaxy	1.1 million mph
6. Overall circular motion of the universe	360,000 mph

Chapter Two

The Bible Was First

Figure #5. A REVOLVING PLANET

A Revolving Planet.

It was not until the 16th century that the idea of the sun revolving around the Earth was replaced with the idea of the Earth rotating daily on its own axis and yearly around the sun. Yet God had explained all of this thousands of years ago to His servant Job.

> Have you ever once commanded the
> morning to appear, and caused the
> dawn to rise in the east? Have you ever
> told the daylight to spread to the ends
> of the earth, to end the night's wicked-
> ness? (Job 38:12,13 LB).

> It is changed like clay *under* the seal
> (Job 38:14 NAS).

The Hebrew word for "changed" carries the
meaning "changed by turning," as in the use of
seals in times gone by.

Seals: Ancient I.D.s.

Seals, symbols of authority, were commonly
used in ancient days for personal identification,
as a driver's license is used today (see Gen.
38:18; I Ki. 21:8; Isa. 29:11). **(See fig. #6.)**

Seals were often made of an engraved, round,
semiprecious stone mounted on a ring. Nearly
everyone had one, and each one was unique.
Each man's ring contained a stone of a different
shape; therefore, it became his personal and
unmistakable signature. **(See fig. #7.)**

For poorer people, cheaper materials were
used, while the well-to-do had the seals made out
of more precious crystals or metals. Thousands

Figure #6. ANCIENT I.D.S

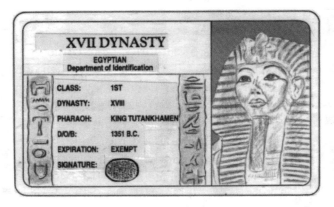

of variations were possible — as with today's
house or car key.

Letters and books were sealed by the writer,

Figure #7. THE ANCIENT SEAL

A SEAL FROM EGYPT

and laws were written on clay tablets bearing the
ruler's seal. The Bible mentions that Judah
carried a seal with him, and that Joseph was
given his pharaoh's seal ring to use. This seal
impression was the equivalent of a signature
today.

In some of the ancient cities, the most

common type of seal was the cylinder. The picture and words would be chosen by the individual, then engraved on a cylinder. When this cylinder was rolled over a bit of soft clay, it left behind a raised image. **(See fig. #8.)** The engraved stone would be pressed into a damp clay tablet, for instance; then the tablet would be turned to form a second impression, resulting in a symmetrical design and circle.

Figure #8. THE CYLINDER SEAL

God Explains How the Earth Turns.

In the book of Job, this raised image represents dawn, the impression left by the sun on the Earth. God paralleled daybreak with the impression left by a signet ring (seal) in clay. The ring (sun) which makes the impression (daybreak) is held in a fixed position, and the clay (Earth), which receives the impression (daybreak), is rotated completely around so the ring (sun) appears in its original position once again. **(See fig. #5.)**

Though He was using figurative language, God was describing to Job a real, physical process. The Bible was indeed first. Long before man ever discovered the axis spin of the Earth, the Bible stated this to be so.

Chapter Three

Atheism Comes Full Circle and Attacks Its Own

Figure #9. THE FLAT EARTH SOCIETY

"ENDS, CORNERS AND PILLARS OF A FLAT EARTH"

Back to the Dark Ages.

Several years ago, *Science Digest,*[3] an evolutionary magazine, carried an article titled, "Is Man Back in the Center?" The question was answered with the statement that some evolutionary scientists believe the Earth really is the center of the universe. The article goes on to say that quantum physics (a theory in physics which deals with the laws governing motion) seem to prove man may really be the focus of creation. Of course, the article does not suggest that the focus on man has any spiritual significance. How amazing!

To question if the Earth is the center of the physical universe seems preposterous in these enlightened times, but for a thousand years the answer seemed to be obviously "yes." As previously mentioned, Ptolemy and a few other Greek philosophers believed that the sun revolved around the Earth. From their position on the Earth, looking up into the sky, that appeared to be the case.

Although several centuries of scientific investigations have given proof to the contrary, some philosophically-minded physicists and others are suggesting once again the Earth is the center of the universe. Earth is indeed the most important planet in the cosmos. In fact, they admit that in a sense creationists are right: Man is at the center. However, their belief is not based on the fact that the Bible says so, but on the theory of quantum physics.

Planet Earth is, no doubt, the most important place in the universe — not because of its physical position, but because it is the spiritual battleground for the forces of evil (Satan) and the forces of good (God).

Pagan Beliefs Rise Again.

More than four centuries have passed since the death of Copernicus and three since that of Galileo. Now the argument between the Church and the atheists is surfacing once again. In recent decades, atheistic humanists have attacked the Church because it once believed the Bible taught the Earth was the center of the universe. Yet today, with the advent of the quantum theory, evolutionists are reverting to Ptolemy's belief that the Earth is the center of the universe. As unbelievable as it may seem, like a shark, the nonbeliever will attack anyone, even his "own." His only concern is to find some way to give meaning to his existence.

However, since neither science nor Scripture support geocentricism (the belief that the Earth is the physical center of the universe), creationists should not consider the recent resurrection of this Dark Ages concept as supporting the

Word of God. It is a theory that leads to scientific weakness and theological error.

It is popular among present-day atheistic humanists to deny any special recognition for the Earth, but we must consider God's Word on the subject. The humanists expound their philosophy that we live on a speck of dust, circling a humdrum star in a far corner of an obscure galaxy. But let it be known, God's Word has stood the test of time, and it declares that man was made in the image of God and given eternal purpose and significance.

Earth, the Battlefield of the Universe.

The Earth and mankind are not an insignificant result of accidental evolution. The Earth is the spiritual reference point of the universe. Christ came to Earth and walked among men, and He will one day return.

There is an unseen spiritual battle going on (Eph. 6:12) for the souls of men and women. It is centered on this planet and extends to high places.

"Why Do I Feel So Lonely?"

Without God, man has no purpose. Without a sense of destiny, he finds himself alone in an impersonal universe. Atheism is spiritual suicide. Some time ago, the press asked the late well-known comedian and skeptic, Groucho Marx, what he thought when the space probe was sent to Mars and was unable to discover any traces of life in the soil. He said, "I feel lonely."

Loneliness is not the result of being alone; rather, it is the result of an attitude of despair and hopelessness. This attitude stems from having no sense of purpose or future in life.

A lack of purpose in life results from either not knowing God or not believing in Him. Without a belief in the Creator, man not only feels lonely, but unnecessary, and he concludes there is no reason for his existence. Only God gives people meaning and purpose.

E.T., Are You Out There?

It is amazing the lengths to which atheists will travel to find justification for their disbelief in God — even to the ends of the universe. This is the case in a May 1996 *Reader's Digest* article titled "Are We Alone in the Universe?" The story tracks astronomers in their pursuit for E.T.

Billions of taxpayers' dollars are being spent annually in hopes of finding a bio-friendly planet with intelligent life on it. The evolutionary motivation for this endless search is revealed in the article: "For those who hope for a deeper meaning beneath physical existence, the presence of extraterrestrial life-forms would provide a spectacular boost." Why a "spectacular boost"?

Because it would be a boost out of a life of meaninglessness. In other words, without God man feels extremely lonely and hopeless.

We Will Probably Never Know.

Bernard M. Oliver, vice president of research at Hewlett-Packard Company, contends that interstellar travel is not a feasible idea.[4] The distances between stars are immense. Even if a crew of astronauts were willing to devote their entire working lives (ages 20-65) to a round-trip visit to the nearest star, they would have to travel at one-fifth the speed of light (37,000 miles per second, or over 130 million miles per hour). At that speed, he says, even microscopic dust can produce a bomb-like impact on the spacecraft — at the equivalent of one pound of TNT per one-thousandth of a gram — which would mean instant disintegration for the spacecraft and its contents.

With that in mind, Earth stands virtually alone in the universe. Man won't be traveling very far from his home by means of 20th-century space travel. Yes, without God, one feels quite lonely in the universe, and the future seems cold and bleak. But to find hope and purpose, all one has to do is open the Bible, which reveals an infinite God Who desires to know each of His creatures in an intimate way.

Chapter Four

The Ends, Corners and Pillars of a Flat Earth

They Never Give Up.

There are numerous biblical passages and phrases that have been brought into question by skeptics in their relentless pursuit to attack the credibility of Scripture. Not only have the passages about the movements of the sun and Earth been challenged, but phrases such as: "the ends of the Earth," "pillars of the Earth," and "four corners of the Earth."

There are those who even link the origin of the "flat Earth" society with Bible-believing saints. They cannot seem to comprehend that writers of the Scriptures used the common expressions of their day. Some of them may not be scientifically accurate, just as many expressions we use today are not. The writers of the Bible were more concerned about communicating spiritual principles than scientific fact.

Nevertheless, some skeptics never give up their unreasonable assaults on Scripture.

We must always remember that our battle isn't against "flesh and blood," but "spiritual forces (rulers) in the heavenly realms" (Eph.6:12). We are involved in the long war of the ages — Satan's struggle with God for the souls of men. His insidious plan is to destroy the love relationship between the Creator and His created beings.

For centuries, these critics of Scripture have contended that the Bible portrays the Earth as the fixed center of the physical universe. They also claim the Earth was viewed by biblical writers as flat and supported by foundations on pillars. Their reasonings were based on scriptural references such as "the ends of the earth" and "the foundations of the earth." But keep in mind, like even modern scientists and engineers do, writers of the Bible often used figures of speech. That they were using metaphors is evident within the context.

When we turn on the evening news and listen to the professional "weather guesser," we hear him use common, everyday figures of speech such as, "The sun will set this evening at 7:32 and will rise at 6:20 tomorrow morning." He knows very well the sun neither rises nor sets. The writers of Scripture likewise used figurative words and expressions that clearly communicated God's message.

Lingo and Jargon. (See fig. #10.)

In every language, there are many phrases and expressions that people do not take literally, but their meaning is understood. For instance, in areas with warmer climates, there is a common request, "Please, crack the window." Obviously, one doesn't break the window. It means to open it slightly to let in a little fresh air. When it rains in Texas, we say it pours "cats and dogs" or it is a gully washer.

"I'm so hungry I could eat a horse." "She's a riot." These are just a few of the many expressions people use which are not scientifically correct, yet we understand their meaning.

"The Pillars of the Heavens."

> The pillars of the heavens quake (Job 26:11).

Skeptics continually reveal their lack of wisdom by proclaiming these figurative passages and phrases in the Scripture as unscientific. They assert the science of Job is primitive and mythological.

For instance, in reference to Job 26:11, they

Figure #10. TEXAS TALK

A

"CRACK THE WINDOWS, PLEASE!"

B

"WOW, IT'S RAINING CATS AND DOGS!"

Figure #10. TEXAS TALK

C

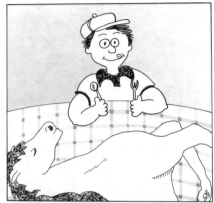

"I'M SO HUNGRY, I COULD EAT A HORSE!"

D

"SHE'S A RIOT!"

argue Job is claiming the mountains of the Earth are pillars holding up the sky like an inverted bowl. They do not realize that the word "pillars" here does not refer to mountains, but to the laws God had put into place to hold things together — the laws of motion, gravity, magnetism, etc. Later in the book God asks Job, "Do you know the laws of the heavens?" (38:33).

Figurative Language of the Bible.

When God inspired the writers of the Word, He led them to communicate in understandable terms. They were free to employ figures of speech to praise Him or to proclaim His message. They obviously inserted lingo and jargon that were common in their day. If this were not so, we would have rivers literally clapping their hands, mountains singing for joy, happy deserts, fields rejoicing and stones crying out. **(See fig. #11.)**

So when the Bible says, "the sun rises and the sun sets" (Eccl. 1:5), it says nothing more than what our meteorologists say, or what our local TV weatherman tells us when he announces the times of tomorrow's sunrise and sunset.

Using a figure of speech does not invalidate science nor does it invalidate Scripture. These expressions add color, warmth and a personal

Figure #11. LET THE WHOLE WORLD REJOICE

touch to each language of the world.

By denying that figures of speech could have been used in the Bible, people at one time believed, and in fact insisted, that the Earth was flat. After all, the Bible speaks of the "four corners of the earth" (Rev. 7:1). Rigid, literal interpretation of this verse would have us accepting that the Earth is a square or rectangular place — with no thickness. For if it had any thickness, there would be eight corners.

The "four corners" are still used as a figure of speech by our news media to represent North, East, South and West. That simply means that the news comes from every direction around the world.

If people are determined to deny the existence of figures of speech in the Bible, they will quickly land in trouble. A literal reading of Scripture is an absolute necessity in understanding it as true, trustworthy and sensible. But we must recognize that in science and Scripture, as in our everyday conversation, figures of speech are commonplace. Walking in Ptolemy's shoes today is not the best way to take a step forward in the progress of science or any other area of education.

Chapter Five

The Sunflower Takes First Place; the Sun, a Close Second

Figure #12. THE SUNFLOWER CAME FIRST

The Sunflower Before the Sun, How Can That Be?

Before we proceed into the account of Joshua's Long Day (Joshua 10) and its focus on the sun, which the Amorites worshiped, it would be worth our time to take a close look once more at the order of events during creation. In doing so, we can see just how comparatively insignificant the sun actually is to the universe and to life. This is important, especially since we know that plants need sunlight to survive, yet they were created before the sun, according to Genesis 1. How could the sunflower survive without the sun?

The Bible declares that the sun was not created until the fourth day, while the plants were created on the third. How can that be? I believe one of the reasons God created in this sequence was to set the record straight for all time. He wanted all generations to understand that as great and powerful as the sun is, it is but a mere whisper compared to God's power. The sun is not the ultimate — God is!

Since ancient times, people have worshiped the sun, and many still do today. The evolutionists consider the sun first in the sequence of life. God, in effect, says, "Not so," and goes on to infer that it isn't even needed for the creation and sustenance of life.

The sun has been given a prominent place in the evolutionary story of creation. But God's story reveals a much different order of events for creation: Life doesn't come from the sun, but from Him.

One of God's Greatest Rivals. (See fig. #13.)

The sun has been one of God's greatest rivals throughout history. Many of the ancient civilizations, such as the Egyptians, worshiped the sun. The

Figure #13. GOD'S GREAT RIVAL

pharaohs claimed that they attained divinity when they became one with the sun-god Ra during an annual religious ceremony. With this in mind, how significant was the dream of Joseph!

> "Listen," he said, "I had another dream, and this time the sun and moon and eleven stars were bowing down to me" (Gen. 37:9).

The Genesis account of Joseph's life is a favorite Bible story. We know that Joseph was a type or shadow of Christ and the Church. He was a savior to Egypt, Canaan and his own family. In Joseph's dream, the sun, moon and eleven stars represented his father, mother and eleven brothers. Through Joseph's faithfulness and God's sovereign providence, the vision came to pass. Figuratively, the sun and moon are types of the previous and current world-system. Just as Pharaoh, who claimed divinity with the sun-god, will one day have to bow to the Almighty God, so it will be with all of creation — everyone will some day bow to the King of kings and the Lord of lords.

The moon only reflects the light of the sun; it has no light of its own. There are many so-called gods and religions who claim to be light and that they have the ability to show the way. Like the moon in Joseph's dream, they, too, will bow to the True Way and Light of the world. It will occur in the last days when the governments of this world will bow and submit to the heavenly authority. Thus the sun, moon and stars will submit to the authority of the Creator God.

The upright Job asserted he hadn't been involved in the worship of the sun as the pagans were; therefore, he questioned why he was suffering (Job 31:26-28). Apparently, the people of his day were involved in sun worship.

God brought ten plagues upon the Egyptians that made a laughingstock of their gods such as the god of the life-giving Nile river. This river was turned into blood and became a stench to the Egyptians' nostrils. God even caused darkness to come upon the land. This was, no doubt, an embarrassment and reproach to their sun-god, Ra.

God in His foresight and wisdom threw an incredible monkey wrench into the whole complex machinery of evolutionism. He created the Earth first, and even the vegetation, before He created the sun.

Matrimony Impossible Between Creation Science and Evolutionism.

There is absolutely no way that one can harmonize the biblical view of creation with evolutionism. But some have tried. In an effort to accommodate the evolutionary theory, some theologians have suggested that each biblical day of creation represents a geological age. One of the principles I learned in my college "Intro to Biology 101" class was that plants like sunlight. If each day of creation represents a geological age, how did the plant world, which was created the day before the sun, survive?

It seems there is a slight difference between the evolutionary account and the biblical account of the creation of the sun, moon, Earth, stars and other planets. The Bible reveals that the Earth was created first and later the sun. Genesis 1:16-19 speaks about the creation of the sun and moon on the fourth day. **(See fig. #14.)**

God's story literally confuses the powers of darkness in whom there is no light. God doesn't need the sun to sustain plant life. God is ultimately the Source of all life. He is the Light of this world. The book of Revelation says in the future there will be no more sun. God doesn't need the sun to maintain time.

> There will be no more night. They will not need the light of a lamp or the light of the sun, for the Lord God will give them light. And they will reign for ever and ever (Rev. 22:5).

Figure #14. THE DISHARMONY OF CREATION AND EVOLUTIONISM

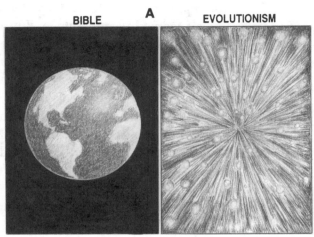

BIBLE   A   EVOLUTIONISM

DAY ONE

BIBLE   EVOLUTIONISM

DAY TWO

Figure #14. THE DISHARMONY OF CREATION AND EVOLUTIONISM

B

BIBLE   EVOLUTIONISM

DAY THREE

BIBLE   EVOLUTIONISM

DAY FOUR

Figure #14. THE DISHARMONY OF CREATION AND EVOLUTIONISM

BIBLE   C   EVOLUTIONISM

DAY FIVE

BIBLE   EVOLUTIONISM

DAY SIX

Night and Day Without a Sun.

Some people ask how God could have divided time into day and night during the first three days of the creation week, as the Bible says He did, if there were no sun or moon. This is really no problem at all, since man has been able to measure day and night without the usual references of sun and moon. Submarines today stay deep in the ocean, often cruising under thick polar ice caps, and no one has any trouble keeping track of the passing of days. Astronauts have stayed in space for months, where there is no day nor night, and they always know what time it is. Even people who lack modern technology have managed to keep fairly accurate track of time, without the aid of any time-keeping device (i.e. those who have been lost in deep underground caves or trapped in mine cave-ins).

Keeping Time Without a Clock.

One man experimented with keeping time without a clock by living in a Texas cave for six months without contact from the outside world and without references to time. He discovered he had a consistent internal clock that told him when to get up and when to go to sleep. With the aid of a computer, he kept track of his daily actions — waking, going to bed, eating, etc.

Nature is full of examples of plants, insects, animals and birds that have internal clocks that function accurately. For example, it's beyond our understanding how the swallows return every spring to Capistrano California Spanish Mission on the same day year after year, but they do. The fact that many species of birds migrate thousands of miles each year to the same place on the same path and on the same date is amazing beyond man's understanding. Yet it happens.

Cycle of Death.

One of the greatest enigmas of time and nature is a fatal cycle. A mysterious "clock" in bamboo has baffled scientists over the years. It determines when the bamboo will die. One Oriental species lives 120 years. Regardless of where they reside in the world, the entire species die together. When the alarm sounds, they flower, seed and die in unison. And nobody knows why. How do the bamboo plants count the years and know when their time has come, even though they are separated by continents? We don't know. But every 120 years in the Orient, the bamboo disaster has been recorded.

Certainly God, Who is all-wise, as well as the Creator of time itself, can keep track of how long a day is without the use of the sun or moon. And since God is the Source of light, He doesn't need the sun to have light. The light in Genesis 1:3 no doubt refers to God, as the sun had not yet been created.

We don't want to "overspiritualize" these verses so that they become unreal. But Revelation tells us that there will be no need for the sun or a lamp in the new Earth after the judgment, for God Himself will be the Light.

Fruit Trees Without the Sun.

In addition, the book of Revelation points out:

> The tree of life, bearing twelve crops of fruit, yielding its fruit every month ... will not need the light of a lamp or the light of the sun, for the Lord God will give them light (Rev. 22:2,5).

In that day, trees will yield fruit without the sun. How will oranges produce vitamin C without the sun? God will be the source of light. God is the Author of time and light. He, then, is the most likely source of light before the sun and stars were created.[5]

Throughout history, the sun has been a stumbling block. Because of its tremendous life-giving power, man, both past and present, has thought it to be almighty. No, God is

Almighty!

About the time someone begins to worship a part of creation, he finds out how rapidly his god can crumble to dust. Yet the evolutionary atheists continue to worship their god of creation — nature. Denying the existence of God, they insist that the Bible is a record of myths.

The account of Joshua's Long Day found in the book of Joshua is proclaimed a classic example of mythology. After all, if God stopped the Earth suddenly, the effect would be somewhat like that of a swiftly moving merry-go-round filled with children being suddenly stopped: The children would fly off. They believe that's what would happen if the Earth came to a sudden halt.

Thus the skeptic believes he has grounds to dismiss God's Word as a fairy tale. But God, in His omniscience, can confound even the atheists and skeptics. The feat He performed for Joshua using the sun literally boggles the mind. But before we look at *how* God might have accomplished this feat from a scientific standpoint, let's look at *why* He did it.

SECTION II
HOT ISSUES ABOUT GOD
AND HIS WORD

Chapter 6: Why Did God Do It?

Chapter 7: Is God a God of War?

Chapter 8: Another Holocaust?

Chapter 9: The Moral Governor of the Universe

Chapter 10: The Moral Depravity Was Beyond Description

Chapter 11: Bringing it Closer to Home

Chapter 12: God's Ultimate Objective

Chapter 13: What About the Women and Children?

Chapter 14: Ample Warning

Chapter 15: The Tragedy of the American Indian

Chapter 16: Time for Housecleaning

Chapter 17: Why Was Israel Chosen as an Instrument of Judgment?

Chapter 18: God is Humane

Chapter Six

Why Did God Do It?

There are a number of miraculous events in the physical realm documented in the book of Joshua. But none are so amazing as the extension of daylight hours. How God accomplished this will be the subject of discussion in Section III. For now, we will investigate why God answered Joshua's request in order that he and his army could destroy the enemy. Why would God do it?

Immediately, a number of hot issues about God and His Word surface. These issues involve God's integrity, His love and His holiness. Is God a holy, just and loving God, or is He a God of war? Why would He command Joshua to "utterly destroy" the inhabitants of the land? (Deut. 20:17 KJV).

Figure #15. GOD OF WAR

Chapter Seven

Is God a God of War?

Check It Out; It's in the Bible.

> The LORD is a warrior; the LORD is his name (Ex. 15:3).

> When the LORD your God has delivered them over to you and you have defeated them, then you must destroy them totally. Make no treaty with them, and show them no mercy (Deut. 7:2).

> In the cities of the nations the LORD your God is giving you as an inheritance, do not leave alive anything that breathes. Completely destroy them — the Hittites, Amorites, Canaanites, Perizzites, Hivites and Jebusites — as the LORD your God has commanded you (Deut 20:16,17).

How could a good God — a God of peace — condone warfare (I Chr. 5:22), give instructions on how war should be fought (Deut. 20), and be acclaimed by His people as a warrior (Ex. 15:3)?

Unfortunately, the film industry has given the public a totally distorted view of the God of the Bible. One such case is the blockbuster motion picture, *Raiders of the Lost Ark*. It is a fictional search-and-find escapade of the lost ark of the covenant, which the children of Israel carried through the wilderness. It eventually came to rest in King Solomon's temple.

The movie portrays God in graphic, high-tech cinematography as a vindictive, angry Almighty, Who disintegrates people who unwittingly violate His wishes such as gazing within the Ark of the Covenant. Viewers are left with the impression that the God of the Bible is like all the other ancient gods of mythology who were often tyrannical and blood-thirsty.

Movies that ridicule the Bible and do injustice to the nature and character of the God of Creation, such as the one mentioned, are released regularly from the film industry. Of course, the bottom line for the movie industry isn't truth about the Almighty God, but bringing in the almighty dollar. Let's consider the rest of the story.

Chapter Eight

Another Holocaust?

The Command to Exterminate.

In Deuteronomy 20:13, the Lord told the Israelites to "put to the sword" every living thing. Why did God command the Israelites to exterminate the people in the land of Canaan? Is this not similar to the Holocaust which the Jews suffered under Hitler's Nazi regime during World War II? How could a loving God command the Israelites to kill everyone, including the little children and the animals as well?

For the answer to be meaningful, we must first believe that God exists. For if God does not exist, there is no problem. The only natural consequences which support and promote Darwin's theory of natural selection — "survival of the fittest" (a tenet of evolutionism) — are war and aggression.

However, if God does exist, then we must believe He has the inherent right to order the Earth and the creatures on it in the way He sees fit.

Some Difficult Questions to Think About.

1. Is it really *good* to stand idly by and not oppose evil?
2. Would a truly *good* surgeon do nothing to cut away the cancerous tissue from a patient and simply allow him to go on suffering until he finally died?
3. Can we praise a police force that offers no resistance to the armed robber, the rapist, the arsonist or any other criminal who preys on society?
4. Could God be called "good" if He forbade husbands to protect their wives and children from murderers?

Goodness Must Oppose Evil.

We must understand that wickedness and crime would run rampant if law-abiding members of society had no right to defend themselves or their families. All possibility of order would be removed. Likewise, God could not be considered good if He were to allow violent criminals to commit atrocities at will or the aggression of invading armies to go unchecked.

Yet one might say that God's command to kill

the peoples of the Promised Land was not a defensive action, but an offensive one. Is this in the same category as premeditated murder? Can it be justified?

It is true that occasionally God commissioned His people to carry out judgment on corrupt and degenerate heathen nations, even to completely exterminate the inhabitants of some wicked cities like Jericho. But as we look closer at the situation, we will see that God's commands were necessary to check the advances of evil or disease, or to judge a nation which was morally and spiritually bankrupt.

Chapter Nine

The Moral Governor of the Universe

God Must Judge Sin.

As the Creator of the universe, God is the moral governor. He is duty-bound to exercise control over all moral beings. He would not be wise and loving if He did not. If a nation insists on breaking God's guidelines for health and happiness, He is responsible to curb that nation's rebellion to prevent pain and misery, or even death.

The world could not long survive if God should cease to exercise judgment on evil nations. God's love requires Him to be just and fair to all His creatures.

But His love encompasses holiness and righteousness, as well as justice. If God failed to exercise judgment, He would cease being a just God. If He ceased being a just God, He would cease being a righteous God. If He ceased being a righteous God, He would cease being a holy God. If He were not holy, He would no longer be a God of love. This is why God is duty-bound to judge a nation that has totally rejected His moral standards. This seems to be the logical explanation for many ancient civilizations coming to a sudden end. Some were wiped out by a natural disaster. Others were destroyed by invading armies.

To think that God is too "nice" to judge sin would be to fail to recognize that God is the moral Judge of the universe. Although God is loving and merciful, He is also just. God will not allow evil to continue unchecked, no matter who the perpetrator is. God punished Israel, His chosen people, when they disobeyed. The doubting and complaining of the generation of Israelites God delivered out of Egypt kept them from being able to enter the Promised Land.

Why Would God Demand Such a "Murderous" Act?

The answer lies in the fact that according to God's standards, the Canaanite nations were grossly immoral and wicked. God's command was not based on the righteous merit of Israel, but in response to the abject wickedness of the Canaanites (Deut. 7:1-11; 9:4,5). Only because of their degenerate and depraved behavior was total destruction needful. Just how wicked were these inhabitants of the Land of Promise? Read the next chapter to find out.

Figure #16. MORAL DEPRAVITY AMONG THE ANCIENTS

Chapter Ten

The Moral Depravity Was Beyond Description

Consider the Evil of These People:

According to God's standards, the Canaanite nations were grossly immoral and wicked. God's use of the Israelites to destroy these wicked people was not based on their righteousness or merit (Deut. 9:4,5; 7:1-11). It was the inordinate degeneration and depravity of the inhabitants of the Promised Land that constrained God to bring total destruction upon them. Scripture describes the hideous perversion in which they were involved.

A Survey of Old Testament Introduction by Gleason A. Archer describes many of the archaeological discoveries concerning the Canaanites. These finds reveal that they were involved in:

1. Polytheism (worship of multiple gods)
2. Sexual perversion (including homosexuality, incest and sodomy)

3. Public, religious prostitution (male and female)
4. Public rites of bestiality (sexual relations between humans and animals)
5. Snake worship
6. Infant sacrifice to the god Molech (believed to be a vicious god who awaited the sacrifice of a living child in his flaming, hollow stomach) **(See fig. #17.)**

More From Leviticus and Deuteronomy.

Because of the Canaanites' wickedness, venereal disease was rampant among the people and the animals alike. The book of Leviticus lists the sins of the pagans resident in the Promised Land: bestiality, homosexuality, incest, adultery, dishonest business practices, murder, witchcraft, sacrificing children to gods and demon worship. There are more listed in Deuteronomy 18:1-8,10-12.

Child sacrifice and occultic practices, which were strictly forbidden by God, were practiced by the people of the land (Lev. 20:2-5). The Lord said that the sins of the people were so gross that even the land was defiled, and it "vomited out its inhabitants" (Lev. 18:25). The Israelites were commanded to replace these hideous practices with worship to the one true God.

Figure #17. MOLECH: A GRUESOME GOD

The moral corruption of these people was appalling. They had become a moral cancer, threatening the continued existence of the nations surrounding them. Cancer must be cut out from every fiber if the body is to be saved. Cutting out a cancer is a serious and delicate operation, but often it is the kindest thing a surgeon can do under the circumstances. God's love and mercy are evident in that He preserved the rest of mankind from the depths of moral pollution to which these nations had sunk.

The command to destroy these nations was both a judgment on them and a safety measure to preserve other nations on the Earth. God was using Israel as His instrument of judgment of evil, just as God would later use other nations to judge Israel for its sins (II Chr. 36:17; Isa. 10:12).

Figure #18. POSSESSING THE LAND

Chapter Eleven

Bringing It Closer to Home

Let's Bring It Closer to Home.

God states in His Word that the whole world belongs to Him (Psa. 50:12; Job 41:11, Ex. 19:5). This means that He can give any part of it to whomever He pleases. We humans are merely stewards of what we have. If we are negligent, then we will forfeit the right to our possessions. Suppose you have been notified by certified mail that you have inherited an estate which includes a beautiful three-story southern-style mansion. The letter informs you that the government repossessed the property from the preceding landlord because he failed to maintain it according to governmental stipulations. Therefore, he forfeited the right to continue to be its owner.

The letter goes on to say that as a result of a drawing, you have been selected as the new owner. The keys and title deed to your mansion are in the envelope.

You call your spouse and children, get in the family car and head out to visit your newly-acquired accommodations. Upon arriving, you see that there is work to be done. The yard is unkempt, several windows are broken, and the mansion needs a new coat of paint.

You proceed up to the entrance and notice that the door is ajar and there is a foul odor coming from the interior. As you peek inside, you are greeted by intoxicated derelicts who appear as though they haven't had a bath in months. In a side room, there are several drug addicts sticking themselves with dirty needles. You ask them what they are doing there, and in reply, they ask you the same question.

You proceed upstairs only to discover prostitutes and homosexuals, and it's obvious that they have contracted AIDS. In the attic, there are all sorts of pornographic garbage, horoscope information, and books on the occult, witchcraft, murder and human sacrifice. Finally, you visit the basement; it is crawling with snakes, spiders and scorpions, and the remains of victims who were sacrificed by occultic devil worshipers are strewn about.

Now let me ask you a question. Would you kindly ask the people living there, "Please move over and make room for my family?" Of course not! To protect your family, you would take whatever measures were necessary to rid the estate of all destructive forces.

Figure #19. WHY THE WALLS CAME TUMBLING DOWN

Chapter Twelve

God's Ultimate Objective

A Closer Look at Jericho.

Archaeology has revealed that the walls of Jericho contained the bones of babies. In that ancient city, infants were often sacrificed to the gods for protection against invading armies. Archaeologists have also identified the remains of microscopic bacteria associated with venereal disease on the remains of both animals and humans. This implies bestiality — humans committing sexual acts with animals.

Because of the recent mad-cow disease which is believed to have killed numerous people who have eaten the infected beef, England may have to eliminate its entire population of adult cows, totalling more than 40 million. How tragic. And yet this helps to explain why God would give the command to eliminate both man and beast. Even domestic animals can be carriers of life-threatening plagues.

The story of Rahab the prostitute (Joshua 2) indicates temple prostitution was an acceptable practice in Jericho. The city was totally perverted. That is why God told Israel to go in and destroy everything.

The Bottom Line.

1. God wanted to stamp out the wickedness of an extremely sinful nation.
2. The wickedness of the people of the land brought about God's punishment.
3. God was using Israel to bring judgment on evil.
4. God wanted to remove all traces of pagan beliefs and practices, and the resulting contamination, from the land.

Furthermore, God's command was designed to protect the nation of Israel from being ruined by the idolatry and immorality of its enemies. What seems to be a ruthless command is in fact an act of love designed to protect the Israelites from moral and spiritual contamination (Deut. 12:31; 18:9-14; 20:18).

Failure to carry out God's command would have resulted in the undermining of Israel's moral and spiritual standards (Deut. 20:16-18). This corrupting influence as a result of Israel's disobedience is apparent in the book of Judges

(Judg. 2:2,3,11-15). So, just as a surgeon who amputates a gangrenous limb is not condemned but praised, thus it should be with God.

Chapter Thirteen

What About the Women and Children?

Children Are Involved in the Palestinian Tragedy.

When Israel became a nation in 1948, the Arabs living there felt they were a people without a country. As a result, the Arab children were displaced and grew up bitter and determined to get their homeland back. Thus one of the worst nightmares in the long Arab/Israeli conflict developed. Terrorist activity has led to thousands of murders over the years. Recently, some Palestinian children have become involved with the suicide bombers that have brought untold misery for both the Jews and the Arabs of Israel. Here is a modern-day example of children being responsible for violence and death. Children are not always innocent bystanders. That may be one reason God ordered the destruction of the Canaanite children.

The Danger of Women.

The Canaanite women were also to be destroyed for they were the ones who had, through the counsel of Balaam, caused the Israelites to be unfaithful to the Lord.

When the Israeli army returned from attacking Midian, Moses asked angrily:

> Have you allowed all the women to live? ... They were the ones who followed Balaam's advice and were the means of turning the Israelites away from the LORD in what happened at Peor, so that a plague struck the LORD's people (Num. 31:15,16).

Apparently, the "plague" was syphilis, gonorrhea or some other contagious and dangerous sexually-transmitted disease. Moses instructed the Israelites to kill all the Midianite boys and the women who were not virgins. Otherwise, the plague could have destroyed Israel.

God's Providential Foresight.

God realized that if the women and children of the land of Canaan, with their evil practices, were permitted to live among the Israelites, misery would follow, and He wanted to spare them. Refugees that come from a depraved society often grow up to be a burden, either morally or economically, and may even be a threat to the peace of a country.

What awaited these children may have been worse than death. Today there are numerous government and religious relief agencies which assist displaced peoples of war-torn areas of the world. In Joshua's day, refugee children were usually abandoned or made into slaves. Long imprisonment is like a living hell. As appalling and sad as it is to see children die of starvation in underprivileged countries, it may be a lesser evil. We must remember this life does not mark the end of man's existence. The wicked often adversely affect the lives of innocent bystanders. As believers, we must do everything within our power to share the Gospel and provide relief to the people who have suffered from the evils of this world.

Today's problems are extremely complex, and the only solution is for the Messiah to return and restore peace to the Earth.

Chapter Fourteen

Ample Warning

The Canaanites Had Received Ample Warning.

From the book of Genesis we learn that one thousand years before this war with the Midianites (a branch of the Canaanites), Noah had pronounced a curse on Ham for his immorality (Gen. 9:25). The Canaanites were the descendants of Ham. In Genesis 19, we find the account of the destruction of Sodom and Gomorrah, which occurred at the time of Abraham. The residents of these two cities were destroyed because of their immorality. This was a warning to neighboring people.

God had warned the Amorites 400 years earlier to repent of their evil:

> Know for certain that your descendants will be strangers in a country not their own, and they will be enslaved and mistreated four hundred years. ...

> In the fourth generation your descen-
> dants will come back here, for the sin
> of the Amorites has not yet reached its
> full measure (Gen. 15:13,16).

God does not judge without due cause. When Israel came out of Egypt, God stated that the nations in the Promised Land were not ready for judgment. Their "cup of evil" was not complete. God is a just God, and He does not judge people unfairly. By Joshua's time, their wickedness and degeneration were irreversible, so that the mercy of God toward Israel and its other neighbors dictated their removal.

The Canaanites Had "Clearly Heard."

In Joshua 2:9-11, we read that the Canaanites had heard about Israel's defeat of over 60 forti-fied cities with the help of its God, yet there is no record of their repentance. The Gibeonites, speaking to the Israelites admitted: "Your servants were clearly told how the LORD your God had commanded his servant Moses to give you the whole land and to wipe out all its inhabi-tants" (Josh. 9:24). Yet there was no sign of humility or repentance.

Finally, we read these unbelievably plain words in Joshua 9:2, "We had CLEARLY HEARD about the coming judgment." The people had clearly heard the amazing story of how Israel had been delivered from the hands of Pharaoh's army, as well as the many miracles of preservation in the wilderness; yet they showed no sign of humility or repentance.

God forewarns mankind time and again before bringing judgment. He did so with the great city of Nineveh through the prophet Jonah, and when the people repented, He showed them mercy. People are without excuse as Romans 1 tells us. God always gives opportunity to repent. He always makes His will clear. The Word tells us that His laws are even written on our hearts.

> For since the creation of the world God's invisible qualities — his eternal power and divine nature — have been clearly seen, being understood from what has been made, so that men are without excuse (Rom. 1:20).

Chapter Fifteen

The Key to Lasting Greatness

Were They "Innocent"? The Tragedy of the American Indian.

Figure #20. AN AMERICAN TRAGEDY

Today, there is a crusade on behalf of the American Indians to try and rectify the stealing of their land and the repression of their culture by the Europeans. There are those who are trying to preserve their traditions and restore their ancient ways. It is true that abuses and atrocities were committed by both sides, and that the Indians did suffer the most. However, the Indians were not innocent victims. Their own pagan practices brought about their destruction. God's Word predicts the judgments of peoples who are involved in evil.

Even if the evil white men hadn't done what they did (and in no way are those actions to be condoned or excused), it was just a matter of time before judgment would have fallen upon the Indians. In fact, archaeology reveals that judgment had already begun to fall long before the white man arrived from Europe. Many tribes disappeared, leaving their villages and their homes — the construction of which revealed incredible ingenuity and considerable labor — without any trace of their whereabouts. No doubt, their disappearance came as a result of disease, drought or other environmental factors. The white men simply continued the process of judgment.

God often brings judgment on wicked people through the hands of other wicked people. For instance, God used Nebuchadnezzar to judge Israel after it turned away from God and began to do evil.

The history of the Indians reveals all sorts of abominable practices such as occultic and demonic worship and the sacrificing of humans. **(See fig. #21.)** God's Word declares that every nation that practices such abominations will be judged.

The Indians of the Americas could not hold on to their accomplishments. The foundation upon which their society was built was weak. It

Figure #21. AN ABOMINABLE CUSTOM

was built on the sand rather than the Rock.
Although of late there has been an attempt to
restore some of their former religious festivals,
they will not make great achievements until they
turn from their occultic ways to the Way, the
Truth and the Life.

Consider Britain.

The British Empire, with its strong Christian
foundation, lasted for more than three centuries.
This super power was at its height of glory at the
beginning of the 20th century. But though
England continues to be a wealthy nation and its
citizens enjoy comfortable lifestyles, the British
Empire no longer rules the world. In direct
correlation to its spiritual decline, Britain has lost
its worldwide sphere of influence. Today there
are pockets of revival throughout England, but it
is no longer a spiritual giant. This nation, which
once sent missionaries and established great
mission agencies in the far corners of the world,
has become spiritually bankrupt, with only about
2% being regular church attenders.

In recent years, England's royal family has
become the tabloids' number one source of
scandalous news. Prince Charles has involved
himself in the religions of the world and declares
that when he takes oath to become England's

next king, he will not "defend the *faith*" (Christianity); rather, he will "defend the *faiths*," as he put it. Not long afterward, the mad-cow epidemic swept through the nation, threatening extermination of the entire country's adult beef population. What has happened to Britain was predicted in the Bible over 2,500 years ago. Idolatry brings the judgment of God.

A Sad Epitaph.

Interestingly, Britain, with its rich spiritual history of anointed ministers who came out of the Reformation, also has a strange and sad aspect. The famous English naturalist, Charles Darwin, was a backslidden seminary student when he wrote his revolutionary, anti-Creationistic book on evolutionism, *The Origin of the Species*. When this infidel died in 1882, he was laid to rest next to Sir Isaac Newton in the famous Westminster Abbey, where great men and women have been buried over the centuries. On the other hand, the great evangelist, John Knox, who led the Protestant Reformation in Scotland in the 1500s, is buried under slot 44 of a parking lot.

It is amazing that the man who made famous a philosophy that directly attacks the foundation of Christianity is honored by being buried in the foundation of the great Westminster Abbey

Cathedral, while the man who stood for the authority of God's Word is buried without honor under a parking lot!

Revelations in Archeology.

The Aztecs, we are told, cut out 1,000,000 living hearts on the sun pyramid located just north of Mexico City. **(See fig. #22.)** The Maya Indians were incredible builders, but they

Figure #22. TEMPLES OF DEATH

heavily practiced human sacrifice and are now virtually extinct. Many statues have been found of a Mayan god believed to be a person holding a bowl for the living hearts of the sacrificed victims. **(See fig. #23.)**

Human sacrifice is an abomination to God and a stench to His nostrils. God says the people who practice such atrocities will be "vomited out" by the land itself (Lev. 18:28). In other

Figure #23. BLOODTHIRSTY GODS

words, judgment will come in the form of pestilence, hurricanes, earthquakes, droughts, fire and other natural disasters.

Just recently, *National Geographic*[6] carried a pictorial story of the discovery of a frozen Inca, the victim of sacrifice high in the Andes Mountains of Peru. The Incas once had an amazing civilization. The massive structures of their cities were erected with such precision that it boggles the minds of engineers today. Yet these highly intelligent people practiced human sacrifice.

God's People Are Not Exempt From Judgment.

God told Israel:

> If you ever forget the LORD your God and follow other gods and worship and bow down to them, I testify against you today that you will surely be destroyed. Like the nations the LORD destroyed before you, so you will be destroyed for not obeying the LORD your God (Deut. 8:19,20).

On the other hand, God promised that if Israel kept His commandments and followed them closely, they would experience His blessings:

> The LORD will make you the head,

> not the tail. If you pay attention to the
> commands of the LORD your God
> that I give you this day and carefully
> follow them, you will always be at the
> top, never at the bottom (Deut 28:13).

It doesn't matter the race or color of a person. Becoming the head or the tail depends upon the choices one makes. A country with righteous-living, missionary-minded citizens will lead the nations. But a land filled with people who delight in sensual pleasures, who are driven to lay up material possessions, and who are concerned only with their own welfare or advantage, is a land set on course for judgment.

The Miracle of South Korea.

An incredible turn of events has transpired in the nation of South Korea. After the Korean War in the 1950s, South Korea was a war-torn Third-World nation. Today, it is fast becoming a powerful industrial nation in Asia. One reason is that South Korea has become a spiritual giant in the Kingdom of God. More than 50% of the people are born again, and it has many churches with membership in the tens of thousands.

Dr. Cho's church, the largest in the world, has a membership of over 700,000. It's amazing how a nation could accomplish so much in such a short time, especially with communism on its doorstep (North Korea). South Korea not only has become a Christian nation, but a praying one as well.

God's Word reveals that those nations that are filled with people who are missions-minded, prayer warriors, obedient to the Word, and friends of Israel, will be blessed.

Chapter Sixteen

Time for Housecleaning

Time Had Run Out.

Joshua and the Israelites were used by God to destroy a wicked empire. The Lord had given the heathen nations in the Promised Land time to clean up their act, but they failed to do so. They would not repent and turn from their evil ways. If they had, as did the citizens of Nineveh, God would have spared them as He did that great city (Jonah 3). Joshua was commanded to destroy the people; otherwise, they would have eventually contaminated the nation of Israel.

It is sad, but the reason God has to resort to total annihilation of a nation, including the children, is that the children become perverted as a result of being influenced by the darkened minds and hearts of their parents. This is why God had to destroy the children of Sodom and Gomorrah and other wicked cities.

The Las Vegas of the Roman Empire.

If you have ever read about the Italian city of Pompeii, it is obvious why it was destroyed by the eruption of Mt. Vesuvius. **(See fig. #24.)** Pompeii's inhabitants were killed by poisonous gas that escaped during the eruption. Having been covered by volcanic ash, Pompeii wasn't discovered until the 19th century. Excavations reveal it was a sin-sick city, much like the city of Las Vegas. Perversion was everywhere. Statues in its public parks depicted gross immorality. The artifacts from the excavations were placed in two museums, one for the public viewing, and one for private viewing, because the contents were X-rated. Statues, mosaics, relics, etc. reveal the city's moral perversion. Las Vegas is nearing the edge of a great judgment, along with so many similar places of evil throughout the world.

Jesus talked about removing the eye and the hand if that will save the person (Matt. 5:29). Doctors understand this important principle. When they have a patient with a gangrenous limb, they know it is necessary to amputate it in order to prevent disease from spreading and killing the person.

**Figure #24. BURIED ALIVE: POMPEII,
CITY OF DEATH**

Figure #24. BURIED ALIVE: POMPEII,
CITY OF DEATH (CONTINUED)

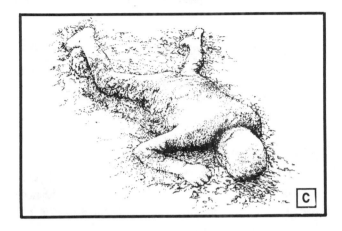

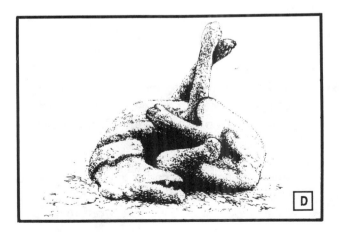

Chapter Seventeen

Why Was Israel Chosen as an Instrument of Judgment?

Why Not a Natural Disaster?

Why did God choose Israel to judge the nations in the Promised Land? Why did He not use pestilence, famine — or natural disaster, as He did with Sodom and Gomorrah? The primary reason is twofold:

1. To be a sharp warning regarding evil practices in the formative stages of the nation of Israel.
2. To be an immediate and a solemn lesson, carrying a deep impression (Deut. 20:18). "The wages of sin is death" (Rom. 6:23).

Chosen for a Purpose.

Israel had been chosen for a great purpose in God's plan of the ages. Israel was to be the nation to whom God would give His Word in written form to be preserved and passed on from generation to generation. In time, the Living Word, the Messiah, the Christ, would step onto the pages of history as a Jew and reveal God's plan of redemption and salvation for all mankind. Israel had a great part in preserving and revealing the greatest story ever told.

As a young nation, Israel was being protected by God from the plan of Satan to destroy it. Satan was well aware of the prophetic words of God in Genesis 3 that in time a Savior would arise to dethrone and strip him of his usurped authority and to redeem fallen man from the clutches of slavery. This is why from the birth of Israel to the present time, Satan has waged an all-out attack against the nation. He is well aware that God is not finished with Israel.

Israel is the nation of destiny. It might well be said, "As the Jew goes, so goes the world." Israel is the yardstick, blueprint, outline and program of God as to what He is going to do in the nations of the world. The land of Israel is called His (God's) land in the Bible.

Israel is the Center of the World.

Geographically, Israel is the navel of the earth, centered between Asia, Africa and Europe. Militarily, politically and economically, it was the hub and crossroads of the ancient world. Today, Israel is the storm center of the entire world and is the location where the last battle, the battle of Armageddon, will be fought.

> I have set you in the middle of the nations (Ezek. 5:5).

Israel was conceived with a miracle. It has survived through miracle after miracle. Egypt couldn't enslave it. The Red Sea couldn't drown it. Jonah's whale couldn't swallow it. The fiery furnace couldn't burn it. Haman's gallows couldn't hang it. And the nations have not been able to assimilate it.

Dictators Cannot Annihilate It.

Israel has experienced unspeakable persecution and unbelievable atrocities at the hands of the pharaoh of Moses' day, Nebuchadnezzar, Alexander the Great, Nero, the Turks, Hitler, the Soviet Union, some of its Arab neighbors, and even some who bear the name "Christian." It can't be destroyed. God is not yet finished with Israel. It is the place where the Messiah, Christ, will return and from which He will rule and reign. Jerusalem will be His home. God created, decreed, loved, called and has protected Israel throughout the centuries.

It Wasn't Israel's Merit.

God's justice is evident: The same warnings given to the heathen were also given to Israel (Lev. 18:26). It isn't due to Israel's merit that it has survived against the odds; rather, God has kept His promise to Israel's ancestors. Just as God chose Israel, He has chosen believers in Christ to be a part of His Kingdom and to rout out the enemy of our souls, Satan.

The Results of Disobedience.

What if Israel had failed to obey God's command? "If you do not drive out the inhabitants of the land, those you allow to remain will become barbs in your eyes and thorns in your sides" (Num. 33:55). God warned Israel that if it didn't obey His command, these wicked people would become a source of great irritation.

That is exactly what happened. Because Israel failed to completely destroy these evil people as God had commanded, it was constantly oppressed by them. Israel's lack of obedience caused them to experience greater bloodshed and destruction than if it had followed God's instructions in the first place.

This is also true of Christians today who are hesitant to clear out all sin from their lives. They do not obey out of fear (their sin seems like a giant) or because it seems harmless or attractive. Hebrews 12:1 tells us to "throw off ... the sin that so easily entangles" us.

In what areas of your life are you struggling? Do you battle a bad habit, an unhealthy relationship, an unrighteous lifestyle, etc.? If you do not overcome these areas of weakness, they will cause you serious problems later and remain as stumbling blocks as you travel the path of life.

Chapter Eighteen

God is Humane

Treatment of Prisoners.

By comparing the laws of God regarding the treatment of prisoners with the actions of the ancient civilizations — including the nations surrounding Israel — toward them, it is obvious that God's care and concern for humanity is far superior. Torturing of prisoners was a common practice by nations around the world.

Notice that God's directions for the treatment of women prisoners of war are remarkably humane (Deut. 21:10-14).

1. There was to be no rape.
2. If a soldier desired a woman, he had to marry her.
3. Soldiers could not make women POWs, slaves or concubines.
4. If a soldier married a POW and later did not want her, he must let her go wherever she liked.

Vengeance is God's.

Furthermore, we read that vengeance belongs to God (Rom. 12:19). Being the Creator of the universe, God is morally responsible to uphold order in it. He will avenge all injustice and wickedness. Since God exhorts us to pray according to His will (I Jn. 5:14), it is right for us to pray that His judgment be visited upon the ungodly — those who have set themselves against God's children.

Unlike the heathen armies who might attack a city without giving it an opportunity to surrender on terms (I Sam. 11:2,3; 30:1,2), the armies of Israel were required by God to grant a city the opportunity to surrender without bloodshed before taking action to destroy them. If they surrendered, they would enter into servitude to the Hebrews.

God's general rule regarding women and children enemy captives was for them to be taken care of and spared from death (Deut. 20:14). There were only occasional exceptions when the enemy was to be completely destroyed because of its total depravity — spiritually, morally and physically.

Spiritual Parallel.

Isaiah 55:7 says, "Let the wicked forsake his

way." Christ taught that we should forgive all who repent (Matt. 18:21,22). He linked repentance with forgiveness when He said that "repentance and forgiveness of sins will be preached in his name to all nations" (Lk. 24:47).

Forgiveness cannot be obtained from God without faith and repentance, which are the means for appropriating God's grace. Thus, if there is no repentance, we should "pray for those who persecute" us (Matt. 5:44). In the Old Testament they prayed, "Do I not hate those who hate you, O LORD, and abhor those who rise up against you? I have nothing but hatred for them; I count them my enemies" (Psa. 139:21,22).

It is not contradictory for God-fearing people to pray for some enemies and against others. We are to pray *for* enemies who do wrong out of ignorance of truth, but *against* those who have set their faces (wills) against God and truth.

God is Not a God of War.

On one hand, God is the Creator, Sustainer and Protector of life:

1. Gen. 9:1,7 — Propagation of life
2. Gen. 8:22; 9:3 — Sustenance of life
3. Gen. 9:2,5,6 — Capital punishment for the murderer, whether animal or human

However, He is a God of war when it is

necessary to remove wickedness and evil. He is a jealous God, and He will protect His own.

God instructed Israel that capital punishment was to be used only in the case of willful, malicious assaults upon the life of another. He even provided cities of refuge for those who had committed manslaughter. God laid down rules of war (Deut. 20) — rules of justice, fairness and kindness in the use of the sword — which truly reflects His goodness.

There are many "hot issues" about God in His Word. We have covered only a few. We must trust that God is just, even if we do not understand everything about Him or His Word. God's Word is truth; it can be trusted for every "hot issue."

Meanwhile, God is always searching for a righteous person through whom He can show His power, might, strength and salvation. He found Joshua, a man of proven character and of steadfast faith.

PART II
JOSHUA'S LONG DAY

SECTION III
HOW DID GOD DO IT?

Chapter 19: Supernaturalistic

Chapter 20: Plotting the Course

Chapter 21: Clue One: Tilt, Tilt, Tilt

Chapter 22: Clue Two: Ancient Lava Flows and Flying Magnetic Saucers

Chapter 23: Clue Three: Earth's Heavenly Attraction

Chapter 24: Clue Four: The Day the Compass Dies

Chapter 25: Clue Five: Heavenly Beach Ball Buddies

Chapter 26: Just for Fun

Chapter Nineteen

Supernaturalistic

On the day the LORD gave the Amorites over to Israel, Joshua said to the LORD in the presence of Israel: "O sun, stand still over Gibeon, O moon, over the Valley of Aijalon" (Josh. 10:12).

The reaction by the skeptical evolutionists to Joshua's "Long Day" is total disbelief. Sarcasm frequently colors their conversation. **(See fig. #25.)** Miracles have no credibility in the mind of the skeptic.

The reason evolutionists deny the possibility of miracles is that they deny the existence of God. To them, the issue is not whether there is evidence for or against the Long Day or the truth of any other part of the Bible; the issue is God's existence. Atheists refuse to accept the existence of God, for to acknowledge Him would mean that they would have to deal with issues such as

Figure #25. JOSHUA AND THE JUDGE

the moral government of God and the eternal consequences for breaking His laws. One of those consequences is hell, the penitentiary of the universe — a place where those who refuse to live in accordance with God's laws of love will be confined forever.

The atheist finds it convenient to refuse to believe there is a God, thereby avoiding dealing with these consequential issues. There is no amount of evidence which could prove a miracle to someone who does not want to believe it can occur. However, there is certainly plenty of reason for Christians, who know God and recognize His power and might, to accept Joshua's Long Day as a fact of history.

Which is Easier, Creating or Adjusting?

Which is easier: creating light or extending the length of daylight hours? Obviously, creating light would be more of a challenge. But for the Creator of the universe, neither is difficult.

The believer should not question if the miracle of the Long Day could or could not have occurred, but *how* it occurred. For God to stop the rotation of the Earth's axis for a time is no more a miracle than for Him to have started the Earth turning in the first place. It is not beyond God's ability and power to stop the Earth from turning in a way that no catastrophic geologic or atmospheric changes would have occurred.

The Merry-Go-Round Effect.

For the God Who created the entire universe out of nothing, why would it be difficult to stop the Earth from rotating without any side effects?

To the skeptic, the supernatural explanation is a bit too much to swallow. After all, anyone can see the difficulties that would arise if the Earth's rotation were suddenly stopped. People, animals — anything not tied down — would go flying, just as children do from a merry-go-round when it is suddenly stopped. **(See fig. #26.)**

However, if the Earth suddenly slowed down, people and loose objects would not fly off into space as one might suspect. In fact, just the opposite would occur. This is because centrifical force (which tends to throw things off the Earth) is only about 1/300th of the strength of gravity. So if the Earth suddenly came to a stop, gravity would actually hold things to the Earth's surface even more firmly.

What About Momentum?

Everyone knows that if a car traveling 100 mph stops suddenly, its occupants will fly through the windshield. But it is also true that the same car can come to a comfortable stop within several seconds. Likewise, if God were to slow the rotation of the Earth, which is traveling at 1,000 mph at the equator, He could do so without any great side effects in just several minutes. Being the Creator, God knows how to do any of the above without causing problems.

Let us consider five clues — natural explanations — as to how God could have used and directed the very laws of the universe that He created to bring about the extra daylight hours needed for Joshua to complete his mission of destroying the Amorite empire.

Figure #26. MERRY-GO-ROUND FACTOR

Figure #26. MERRY-GO-ROUND FACTOR

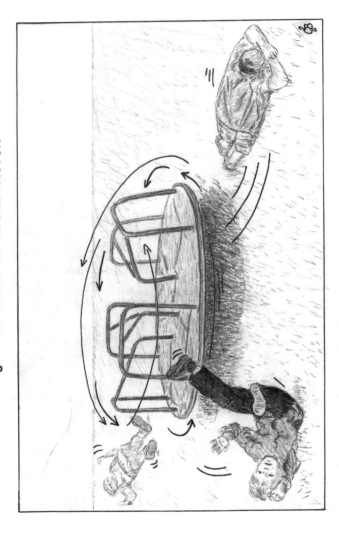

Chapter Twenty

Plotting the Course

The Sun-God Assisted in the Destruction of the Amorites.

The Amorites, who dwelt in the Promised Land, were enemies of Israel. History reveals that the Amorites were sun worshipers who committed all sorts of terrible atrocities. God had given them plenty of opportunity to humble themselves, as He did with the city of Nineveh, yet they had not responded. Now it was time for judgment, and He planned to destroy them.

God uses numerous ways to judge evil nations. He can cause a natural disaster — a drought, an earthquake, a volcanic eruption, tsunami (gigantic waves), a plague, a fire, a scourge of insects, or even a shower of meteorites. On this occasion, He not only used the nation of Israel, but incorporated into the judgment a miraculous event using the very thing the Amorites worshiped: the sun. God supernaturally provided the additional daylight Israel needed to complete its conquest over the Amorite forces before they could escape and regroup during the night hours.

Charting the Skies.

> O sun, stand still over Gibeon, O moon, over the Valley of Aijalon (Josh. 10:12).

Looking at a map of Palestine **(see fig. #27)** at the time of Israel's conquest, one can visualize the setting: Joshua and his army marched all night from the west, Gilgal. They met the Amorites at Gibeon, where God gave Israel victory.

One must engage in astronomical gymnastics to sort out the exact positions of the sun and moon at this point, depending upon how one interprets Scripture. The bottom line is, "The sun ... delayed going down about a full day. There has never been a day like it before or since. ... Surely the Lord was fighting for Israel" (Josh. 10:13,14).

Figure #27. PLOTTING THE COURSE

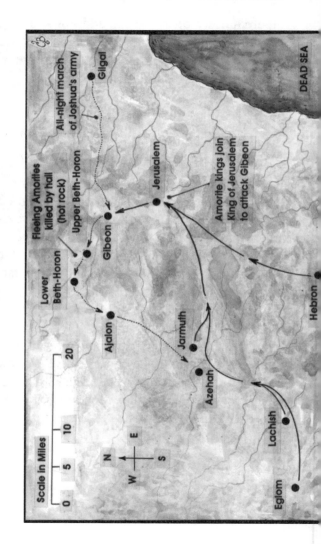

Figure #28. TILT, TILT, TILT

Chapter Twenty-One

Clue One: Tilt, Tilt, Tilt

A Lesson From Pinball Machines.

Why are summer days longer than winter days? The answer is: tilt, tilt, tilt. If you are puzzled, consider the following illustration.

Pinball machines have provided the public with entertainment for decades. Players know that when the "tilt" light flashes the game is over. The light flashes when a player hits the side of the machine in an attempt to redirect the ball to score extra points or to keep the ball from exiting in order to extend play time. The problem occurs when the player jostles the machine too strongly. The result is a penalty: The machine flashes "tilt," and the game is over.

This illustration can help in understanding why daylight hours are extended during the summer months: The Earth is tilted. Who or what jostled or tilted the Earth in order to "extend play" for Joshua's army?

The Clue From the Months of Summer.

What causes the extended hours of sunlight at the North Pole during the summer months? It's the tilt of the Earth in relation to the sun. The Earth is slightly tilted at $23\frac{1}{2}°$ between the North and South Poles. **(See fig. #29.)** As the Earth

Figure #29. THE EARTH'S ANGLE

23 1/2°

orbits the sun, the tilt and position of the North Pole changes from pointing toward the sun to pointing away from the sun. **(See fig. #30.)**

When the North Pole points toward the sun, the summer months, with their additional daylight hours, occur in the Northern Hemisphere. In fact, for four months of the year the sun never sets above the Arctic Circle. **(See**

Figure #30. SEASONAL SHIFTS

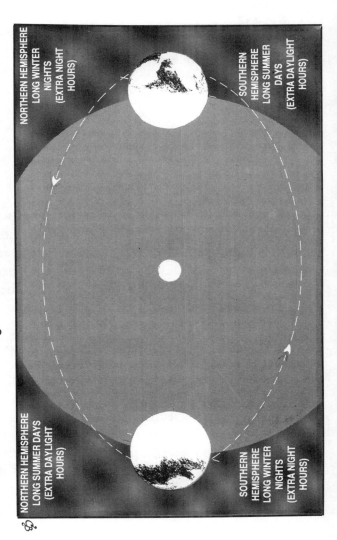

fig. #31.) It is still visible, even at midnight. **(See fig. #32.)**

Six months later, the Earth is on the opposite

Figure #31. ARCTIC CIRCLE

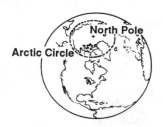

side of the sun, and the North Pole is facing away from the sun. This results in the winter months, with the longer night hours. For those several months, the sun never rises above the horizon. On the other end of the earth, the Southern Hemisphere experiences just the opposite of what the Northern Hemisphere does.

All this occurs as a result of the $23\frac{1}{2}°$ tilt of the Earth as it orbits around the sun. Thus, the tilt of the Earth is the cause of additional sunlight during the summer months.

The above scientific information provides insight as to how the laws which govern the Earth's tilt and rotation may have been affected to bring about the additional daylight hours the Word of God tells us were supplied during

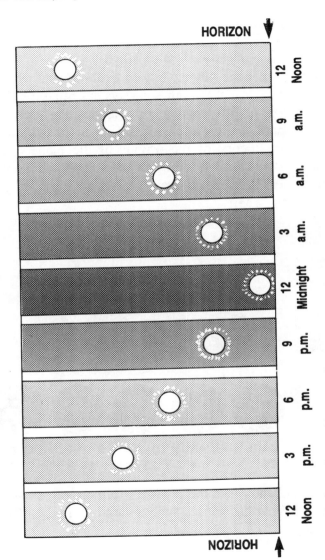

Joshua's Long Day.

The Celestial Pinball Machine.

It must be puzzling to evolutionists why all nine planets in our solar system rotate on their axis at different degrees of angles. Presently, the Earth is tilted at 23.45°. Based on the evolutionary theory of the origins of the planets, one would think that they should all be tilted more or less the same. However, this is not the case. **(See fig. #33.)**

Mercury's axis stands perpendicular, while

Figure # 33. PLANETARY TILTS

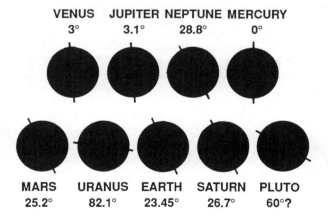

VENUS	JUPITER	NEPTUNE	MERCURY
3°	3.1°	28.8°	0°

MARS	URANUS	EARTH	SATURN	PLUTO
25.2°	82.1°	23.45°	26.7°	60°?

Uranus is tilted at 82.1° (almost on its side). What has caused such a variation in the tilts of the planets? It appears that the solar system represents an immense celestial pinball machine.

Apparently, there have been numerous occasions during the 6,000-year history of our solar system in which major tilts (catastrophic events) have taken place, resulting in the variation we see throughout the planetary system.

Summary of Clue One: The tilt of the Earth is the reason for extended daylight hours in summer.

Chapter Twenty-Two

Clue Two: Ancient Lava Flows and Flying Magnetic Saucers

Earth in Upheaval and Worlds in Collision.

The late Immanuel Velikovsky was a Jewish scientist who wrote a number of scientific books. He believed that many of the catastrophes mentioned in the Old Testament were the result of heavenly objects entering the atmosphere and falling to the ground. He associated the Old Testament judgments on nations with activities of heavenly bodies. He even suggested that some of the plagues of Egypt were caused by the interaction of planetary forces which occurred when a stray planet came close to the Earth at the time of the Exodus.

Two of Velikovsky's books, *Earth in Upheaval* and *Worlds in Collision*,[7] document his research. For many years, he was considered an extremist by other scientists. For one reason, he made some unusual claims about Venus' age and makeup. Evolutionary scientists derided his ideas. But when U.S. space probes sent back pictures and data from Venus, his views were confirmed.

Velikovsky believed Venus was relatively young compared to the other planets. This was totally contrary to evolutionary beliefs that Venus is 4.6 billion years old. Amazingly, NASA's probe, Magellan, sent back pictures which revealed that the planet has a shortage of craters. If it is as old as evolutionists believe, it should be covered with craters like the other planets in the solar system.

Do you think that this evidence has changed the minds of evolutionists? Of course not! Evolutionists *have* to believe it is four-and-a-half billion years old in keeping with their theories. They are presently searching for the imaginary force that has erased the craters from the surface of Venus (*Discovery*, January 1992).

Nevertheless, Velikovsky's opinion has now been confirmed as fact. Many scientists now consider Venus to be much younger than the rest of the planets.

Velikovsky also had some unorthodox views regarding Joshua's Long Day. He believed that the extended daylight was brought about by the laws of physics which govern heavenly bodies when they come into one another's realm of influence. Could heavenly objects influence the Earth, causing additional sunlight such as occurred on Joshua's Long Day?

Could Velikovsky's convictions once again be correct? A clue that would suggest Velikovsky's views are correct have been found among ancient lava flows.

Ancient Volcanic Lava Flows Provide a Clue.

When volcanoes erupt, the lava that flows out contains tiny magnetically-charged particles called iron ions which act like compasses. Normally, when these iron ion particles cool, the magnetic aspect within each particle is frozen (hardened) pointing to the magnetic North Pole.

However, there are ancient lava eruptions in which the particles do not point to the magnetic North Pole, but toward the sky. **(See fig. #34.)** This suggests that there was some strong magnetic source in the heavens at the time of the eruption. It attracted these tiny particles of lava, causing them to harden pointing heavenward rather than toward the North Pole.

Here's an illustration. If you were to hold a compass in your hand, it should point to the magnetic North Pole. However, if you were to

Figure #34. POINTING HEAVENWARD

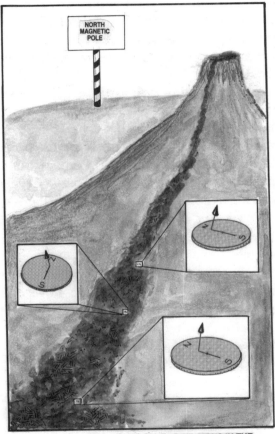

LAVA FLOW   MICROSCOPIC IRON IONS IN THE
HARDENED LAVA POINT HEAVENWARD
RATHER THAN TOWARDS THE MAGNETIC
NORTH POLE

bring a strong magnet close to the compass, the power of the magnet would override the attraction of the magnetic North Pole. As a result, the needle would spin rapidly until it fastened itself in the direction of the magnet. (**See fig. #35.**)

Thus these tiny lava particles pointing heavenward suggest that at the time of the eruption there was some object in the sky causing them to cool pointing upward. What could have caused them to point heavenward? Perhaps a flying magnetic saucer — or possibly a stray planet with a magnetic field like that of the Earth's.

Summary of Clue One: The tilt of the Earth is the reason for extended daylight hours in summer.

Summary of Clue Two: There are magnetic properties in some ancient lava flows which point heavenward instead of toward the magnetic North Pole, indicating that during some eruptions of long ago, there was something unusual in the heavens.

Figure #35. MANIPULATING MAGNETIC NEEDLES

A

B

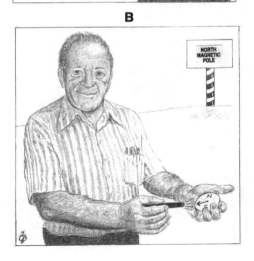

Chapter Twenty-Three

Clue Three: Earth's Heavenly Attraction

Figure #36. INVISIBLE FORCES

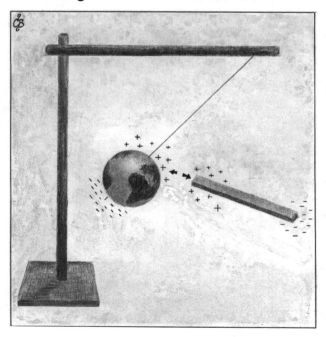

The Power of Magnets.

Magnets have always fascinated people, probably because they possess an invisible power which seems to defy gravity. The force of a strong magnetic bar of iron is capable of suspending objects in air and moving them about as if the law of gravity has been momentarily suspended.

Some archaeologists believe that the ancients possessed the knowledge and capability to move giant stone blocks and statues weighing tons by utilizing the force of magnetism. Although this is only speculation, there is significant research being conducted on the use of magnetism[8] to move objects. If the ancients were able to move such large objects, it may have been accomplished in association with occultic powers.

The Magnetic Earth.

Surrounding the Earth today is the magnetic belt. Man has learned to use this belt to aid in navigation. This belt acts as a powerful, invisible shield against radiation from the sun and outer space.

The magnetic shield of the Earth represents a third clue and key factor in understanding how God could have provided additional daylight for Joshua. The magnetic field that surrounds our planet is caused by an enormously potent magnet running through its center. **(See fig. #37.)** The

Figure #37. EARTH'S MAGNETIC CENTER

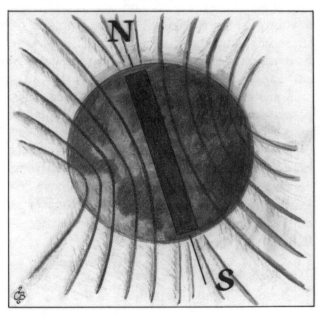

magnetic North Pole is the positive end and the magnetic South Pole is the negative end. This magnetic field has a powerful influence that can affect other heavenly objects that come near the Earth. Most other planets and heavenly bodies also possess a magnetic field. As a result, the magnetic field of one heavenly body can affect another if it comes close. Amazingly, this attraction is so powerful, that a heavenly body can disturb the orbit and rotation of a planet.

Messing With Magnets.

Have you ever played with magnets? One magnet can be manipulated by another without the two ever touching because of the strong magnetic field that each possesses. When two poles are the same, they repel one another; when they are opposite, they attract one another.

The force of toy magnets varies, and usually two that are stuck together can easily be separated by a child. However, today's technology can make a simple electric magnet using a $1\frac{1}{2}$-volt flashlight battery to produce a magnetic strength equal to 500 pounds of pressure. Neither a child nor an adult can separate those two magnets. This power is so great that a 250-pound adult holding a 100-pound child in each arm, with 50 pounds to spare, could hang upside down from a crane supported by this simple magnet. **(See fig. #38.)**

The power of magnets is amazing. Can you imagine the tremendous strength of the huge magnet that runs through the Earth? Satellites which circle the Earth can detect the strength of the magnetic field and give a visual image of the

Figure #38. THE POWER OF MAGNETS IS AMAZING

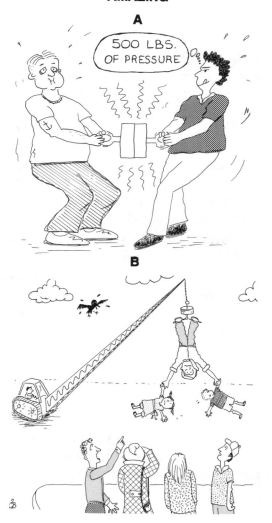

enormous expanse of its influence in space. **(See fig. #39.)** It extends up to 50,000 miles into

Figure #39. EARTH'S MAGNETIC FIELD

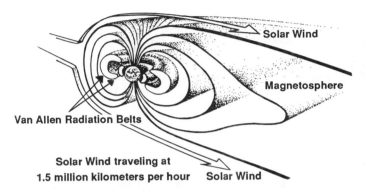

Solar Wind

Magnetosphere

Van Allen Radiation Belts

Solar Wind traveling at
1.5 million kilometers per hour   Solar Wind

space. Its influence is immense, but it was even stronger in the past. Like everything in the universe, the Earth's magnetic field is decaying and growing weaker.

Summary of Clue One: The tilt of the Earth is the reason for extended daylight hours in summer.

Summary of Clue Two: There are magnetic properties in some ancient lava flows which point heavenward instead of toward the magnetic North Pole, indicating that during some eruptions of long ago, there was something unusual in the heavens.

Summary of Clue Three: The Earth is a gigantic magnet.

Chapter Twenty-Four

Clue Four: The Day the Compass Dies

The Decaying Magnetic Field.

Physicist Dr. Thomas Barnes, professor of physics at the University of Texas, has stated that the Earth's magnetic field has been regularly decaying since it was first measured in 1835. Measurements taken over the past 130 years record a 14% decrease in power.

Dr. Barnes reveals that the strength of the magnetic field has a half-life of 1,400 years, so every 1,400 years its strength decreases by half. According to observations, it is predicted that the magnetic field will virtually vanish as early as 3180[9]. In other words, after the year 3180, Boy Scouts will have to use something else besides a compass to help them find their way through the woods during their wilderness expeditions.

The Day the Compass Was Alive and Well.

Had Joshua had a Boy Scout compass handy, it would have worked exceedingly well. Dr. Barnes points out that calculating backward, the strength of the Earth's magnetic field was twice as intense every 1,400 years. In other words, 1,400 years ago, it would have been twice as strong as it is today. In 825 B.C., it would have been four times greater than it is today. When Joshua was alive (approx. 1400 B.C.), it would have been around six times stronger than it is today. **(See fig. #40.)**

If man-made magnets can be so powerful, imagine the potency of the magnetic force when Joshua was alive — six times stronger than it is today. Had Joshua been as far away as the moon with a compass, it could have shown him in which direction the magnetic North Pole was on planet Earth.

The fact that Earth once had a stronger magnetic field means it would have had a greater influence on a heavenly object with a magnetic field that may have come near and vice versa. As fantastic or preposterous as it may sound, there are powerful forces in the heavens which can alter the tilt of the Earth's axis. This, in turn, could provide additional hours of daylight which occurred during Joshua's Long Day.

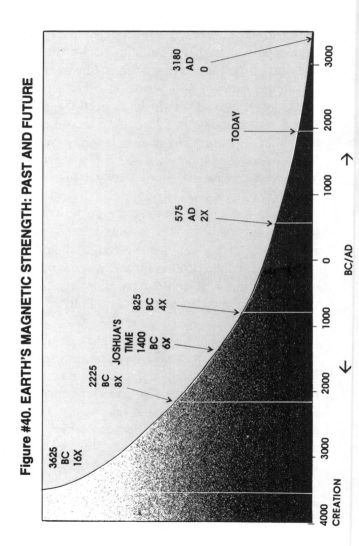

Figure #40. EARTH'S MAGNETIC STRENGTH: PAST AND FUTURE

Summary of Clue One: The tilt of the Earth is the reason for the additional daylight hours in summer.

Summary of Clue Two: There are magnetic properties in some ancient lava flows which point heavenward instead of toward the magnetic North Pole, indicating that during some eruptions of long ago, there was something unusual in the heavens.

Summary of Clue Three: The Earth is a gigantic magnet.

Summary of Clue Four: The Earth's magnetic field was six times stronger during Joshua's day than it is today.

Figure #41. MAGNETIC BEACH BALLS

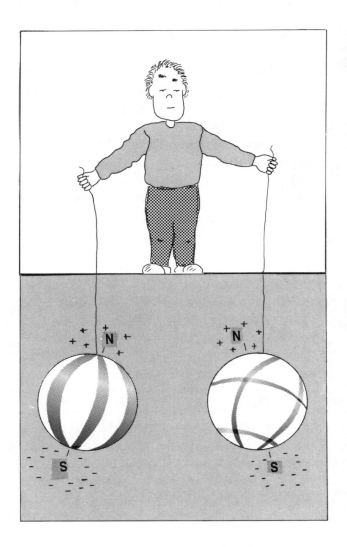

Chapter Twenty-Five

Clue Five: Heavenly Beach Ball Buddies

Magnetic Beach Balls.

Imagine two large beach balls side by side, each suspended in air by a string. Each ball has a magnetic north and south pole. What do you think would happen if you were to bring one ball near the other? Depending upon the strength of the magnets, the interplay between the balls could result in a number of unusual, bizarre and erratic movements. **(See fig. #42.)**

Now enlarge your frame of reference to the heavens. What would happen if another heavenly body were to pass within the sphere of the Earth's magnetic field? If the body had a magnetic field, its invisible force could cause Earth to experience a number of bizarre and erratic movements — fluctuations, orbital shifts, axis shifts, rotational shifts, and a wobbling after-effect as it moved in its path around the sun.

Figure #42. BIZARRE BEACH BALLS

A

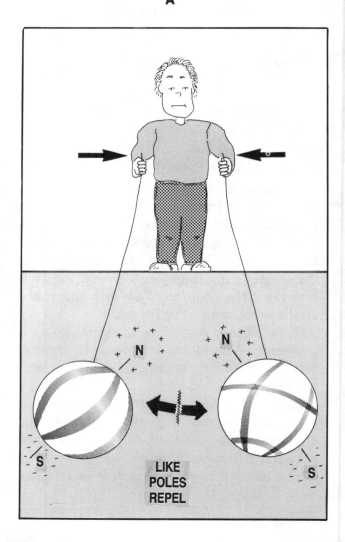

Figure #42. BIZARRE BEACH BALLS

B

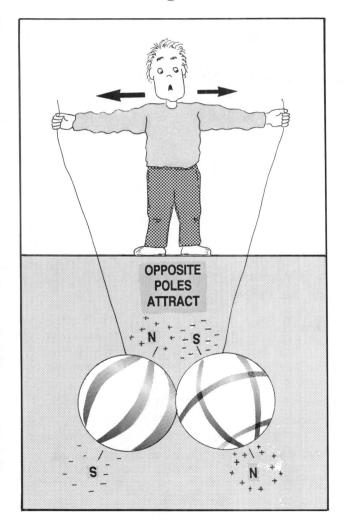

The extent of the effect would depend upon the strength of its magnetic field and how closely it passed by the Earth.

An Unearthly Earth.

Have you ever seen a model of the Earth which could be suspended in the air without any strings attached? I have a world globe (about the size of a basketball) that can be suspended in air by electric magnets. **(See fig. #43.)** The globe can actually be spun while it hovers in midair between two magnets. When a strong magnet is brought near the globe's magnetic pole, it can actually cause the globe to be perturbed, triggering it to move erratically. When the magnet is brought too close, it can actually dislodge the globe from its position. The disturbance is simply caused by a stronger magnetic field coming near it. **(See fig. #44.)**

Heavenly Magnetic Attraction.

Under the right conditions, the same phenomena could occur with planet Earth as a result of another heavenly body with its own magnetic field passing within the Earth's magnetic field. Since magnetic fields like the Earth's have been discovered in most of the other planets, and because of certain indications in God's Word, we

Figure #43. A MINIATURE MAGNETIC GLOBE

have reason to suspect that at least at one point in the history of our solar system, some heavenly object did come near the Earth. **(See fig. #45.)**

The object's magnetic field could have disturbed the Earth's magnetic field, causing the Earth to

Figure #44. MANIPULATING MAGNETIC FIELDS

increase its tilt toward the sun so that Joshua received more daylight hours. This is not difficult to accept as plausible, since the tilt of the Earth presently causes additional daylight hours in the Northern Hemisphere during the summer months.

Figure #45. CLOSE ENCOUNTERS OF A HEAVENLY KIND

As unearthly as it may seem, we now have a reasonable explanation for Joshua's Long Day. And we are using the very laws which govern our planets — laws which were created by God and are at His disposal.

Summary of Clue One: The tilt of the Earth is the reason for extended daylight hours in summer.

Summary of Clue Two: There are magnetic properties in some ancient lava flows which point heavenward instead of toward the magnetic North Pole, indicating that during some eruptions of long ago, there was something unusual in the heavens.

Summary of Clue Three: The Earth is a gigantic magnet.

Summary of Clue Four: The Earth's magnetic field was six times stronger during Joshua's day than it is today.

Summary of Clue Five: The magnetic field of a heavenly body, when it comes within another heavenly body's field of influence, can cause that body's angles or axis to fluctuate and tilt.

Now we have the making of another chapter from *The Original Star Wars and the Age of Ice*.[10]

Chapter Twenty-Six

Just for Fun

Try an Experiment.

The extra daylight that Israel received on Joshua's Long Day can easily be demonstrated with a strong flashlight and a globe that can revolve and tilt more than $23\frac{1}{2}°$. Face the globe so that it can be tilted toward the sun (flashlight). Starting with Israel on the daylight side, begin to slowly rotate the globe to the right to simulate the daylight hours upon the Earth. **(See fig. #46A.)**

As the Earth revolves, the nation of Israel will begin to move from facing the flashlight (sun) to the dark side of the Earth. But just as the light of the flashlight begins to disappear from the country of Israel, begin tilting the globe toward the flashlight as you continue to slowly rotate it.

Notice the more you tilt the globe, the more light reaches the back side toward the equator. **(See fig. #46B.)** There you have it. You have

Figure #46A. SIMULATING JOSHUA'S LONG DAY

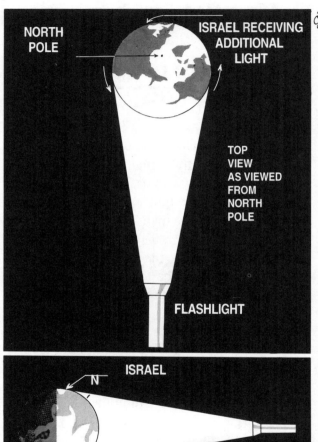

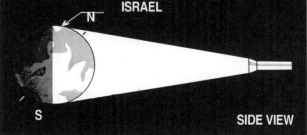

Figure #46B. SIMULATING JOSHUA'S LONG DAY

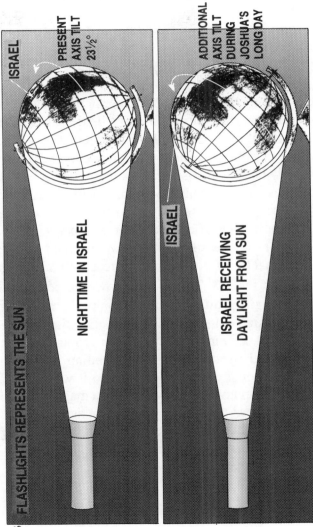

provided additional daylight hours for the countries in the Northern Hemisphere on the back side of the globe, which includes Israel. You have provided Joshua with additional daylight to fight the Amorites.

The Problem Resolved.

Now we can see that the extended daylight that occurred during Joshua's battle could have come about as a result of the interaction of the Earth's magnetic field with that of another heavenly body with a similar magnetic field.

As the heavenly body approached Earth, the two bodies' magnetic fields would have disturbed and affected each other's axis. (See fig. #47.) This easily could have resulted in the normal tilt of the Earth to increase slightly from its normal $23\frac{1}{2}°$ axis tilt, providing additional daylight hours so that Joshua's military campaign could be completed. (See fig. #48.)

Just as magnets are either attracted to or repelled by one another, depending on which poles come near one another, so it would be if another planetary body that had a magnetic field came near the Earth. The two magnetic poles would either be attracted to each other, causing each to tilt toward the other, or be repelled, causing them to tilt away from each other.

Figure #47. TRACKING THE HEAVENLY VISITOR

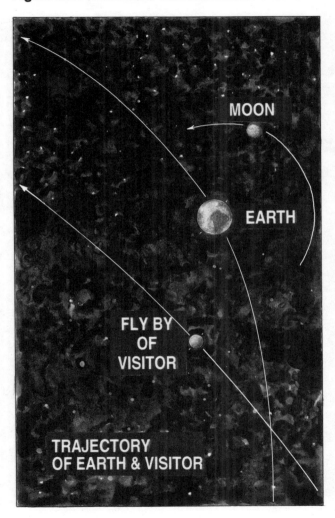

Figure #48. AXIS SHIFT

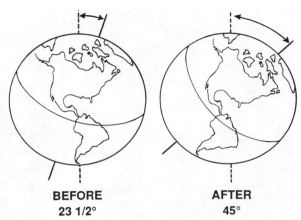

BEFORE
23 1/2°

AFTER
45°

As amazing as this may sound, who is to say that it didn't happen this way? And there is more to the story that confirms that such an explanation is not only reasonable, but highly probable. Our story continues in the following chapter, *Hot Rock From Heaven*.

Section IV
LOOK UP FOR YOUR JUDGMENT
DRAWETH NIGH

Chapter 27: Hot Rock From Heaven

Chapter 28: "Floodgates of the Heavens"
(Heavenly Fallout)

Chapter 29: The Formation of Meteorites

Chapter 30: Exploding Heavenly Bombs
and Other Biblical Catastrophes
From Above

Chapter Twenty-Seven

Hot Rock From Heaven

Hailstones: Ice or Rock?

We now continue to build upon the premise that something was taking place in the heavenlies during Joshua's Long Day. As previously mentioned, the extended daylight hours which occurred during Joshua's battle could have easily been caused by the interaction between the Earth and another heavenly body with a similar magnetic field. As the the body approached Earth, the two magnetic fields would have disturbed and affected each other, resulting in the Earth's axis tilt fluctuating and causing additional daylight hours in some parts of the world.

Not only was the angle or tilt of the Earth affected on Joshua's Long Day, but apparently, there were also adverse earthshaking events occurring. Joshua 10 and the Talmud reveal that at the same time the Israelites received the extra daylight they needed, the Earth was quaking and hailstones were falling, killing more of the enemy than the Israelites did. This indicates the significance of this section's title: *Look Up for Your Judgment Draweth Nigh.* (**See fig. #49.**)

> The LORD threw them into confusion before Israel, who defeated them in a great victory at Gibeon. Israel pursued them along the road going up to Beth Horon and cut them down all the way to Azekah and Makkedah. As they fled before Israel on the road down from Beth Horon to Azekah, the LORD hurled large hailstones down on them from the sky, and more of them died from the hailstones than were killed by the swords of the Israelites (Josh. 10:10,11).

Meteorites and Earthquakes.

This passage indicates that something, perhaps an earthquake, "threw them into confusion." In fact, in its record of this event, the Jewish *Talmud*, a book of Jewish tradition, indicates an earthquake did occur.[11]

Then great hailstones fell from the heavens, killing more of the enemy than the swords of the Israelites did. The Hebrew word "barad" is transliterated into English as hailstones. Because

Figure #49. HOT ROCK FROM HEAVEN

the King James translators (1611) did not fully understand astronomical phenomenon, they have translated "barad" in more than a dozen ways in the English Bible: plagues, tumults, brimstone, hailstones, pestilence, murrain and lightning. No matter how our Church fathers translated "barad," the bottom line is that it meant there was disaster. Many of the passages where the word "barad" is found may in fact indicate there was meteorite activity.

Frozen Snowballs or Hot Rock?

Even today, newer translations do not do justice to the full meaning of "barad." No doubt the scholars who have served on the teams of translators have had a limited understanding concerning cosmic catastrophe. Hailstones is a valid translation as long as it doesn't mean frozen water; however, the general public normally assumes "hailstones" to mean something "composed of ice."

Another meaning to the word "barad" is "hot rock." Some additional passages which use "barad" are as follows. Consider the words that are associated with "barad."

1. "At the brightness *that was* before him his thick clouds passed, **hail** *stones* (barad) and coals of fire. The LORD also thundered in

the heavens, and the Highest gave his voice; **hail** *stones* (barad) and coals of fire" (Psa. 18:12,13 KJV).

2. "And the LORD shall cause his glorious voice to be heard, and shall shew the lighting down of his arm, with the indignation of *his* anger, and *with* the flame of a devouring fire, *with* scattering, and tempest, and **hailstones** (barad) (Isa. 30:30 KJV).

3. "So the LORD sent a **pestilence** (barad) upon Israel from the morning even to the time appointed (three days): and there died of the people from Dan even to Beersheba seventy thousand men" (II Sam. 24:15 KJV).

4. "And I will plead against him with **pestilence** (barad) and with blood; and I will rain upon him, and upon his bands, and upon the many people that *are* with him, an overflowing rain, and great **hailstones** (barad), fire, and brimstone" (Ezek. 38:22 KJV).

5. "Before him went the **pestilence** (barad), and burning coals went forth at his feet" (Hab. 3:5 KJV).

Notice the close association between the hailstones and the coals of fire, flames of fire, brimstone and pestilence coming down from heaven. It is remarkably apparent that judgment was associated with destruction from the heavens, and the form of devastation was caused by hot meteoric material.

In the final section of this volume, we will take a closer look at passages in the New Testament which speak about the coming events associated with the end of the age. It appears that many of those events will again be associated with destruction coming from the heavens. We only mention here that there are 100-pound hailstones mentioned in Revelation 16:21. No doubt these refer to meteorite rocks. From whatever they are composed, they are going to come out of the sky and will be lethal.

For now, let's continue to look at what was happening in Old Testament times. Not only was fallout from the heavens occurring during Joshua's day, but during Isaiah's time as well.

Chapter Twenty-Eight

"Floodgates of the Heavens"
(Heavenly Fallout)

Figure #50. HEAVENLY FALLOUT

Isaiah's Catastrophic Perception.

The Old Testament prophets give us a vivid picture concerning catastrophic events which occurred during the history of Israel from the time of the Flood until the Babylonian captivity (approximately 2500 B.C. to 500 B.C.). In particular, Isaiah gives many helpful insights to such events and helps us to understand phrases like, "floodgates of the heavens," "mountains skipped like rams," and "pit and snare."

"Floodgates of the heavens" (Isa. 24:18) probably refers to the bombardment of meteoric matter. "Mountains skipped like rams" (Psa. 114:4) refers to the undulating (rolling) of the Earth — the rising and falling of the crust of the Earth caused by internal quaking. No doubt, pits or cracks appeared on the Earth's surface as it folded and undulated during earthquake activity.

With these thoughts in mind, let us take a look at a passage in Isaiah which refers to the judgments coming from the heavens.

The Snare and the Pit.

> Terror and pit (crack or opening in the ground) and **snare** await you, O people of the earth. Whoever flees at the sound of terror will fall into a **pit**; whoever climbs out of the pit will be

> caught in a **snare**. **The floodgates of
> the heavens are opened** (Isa.
> 24:17,18).

Notice the word "snare." The passage reveals that whoever climbs out of the pit or crevice in the Earth, no doubt from earthquake activity, will be caught by a snare. What is the meaning of the snare? In Psalm 11:6 we find the meaning of the word "snare" by the words which are associated with it:

> Upon the wicked He will rain
> SNARES, FIERY COALS AND
> BURNING SULFUR; a scorching
> wind will be their lot.

The same Hebrew word is translated into English as "snare" in Isaiah 24:18 and Psalm 11:6. The verse in Psalms also contains "fiery coals and burning sulfur" coming from the heavens. In other words, hot meteorite rock was falling.

At this point, we need to ask ourselves a few questions. Now that we know that snares are associated with hot rock from heaven, where did they originate? Does God have a heavenly gravel pit? When He's ready to hurl some hot rock toward Earth, does He simply command a few angels to scoop them up and do the dirty work? Not hardly, because there is an abundance of meteorite material at His disposal in the heavens.

Chapter Twenty-Nine

The Formation of Meteorites

Asteroid Belt.

Between Mars and Jupiter exists a ring of rocks completely encircling the sun. The ring is known as the asteroid belt. (See fig. #51.) From where did

Figure #51. ASTEROID BELT

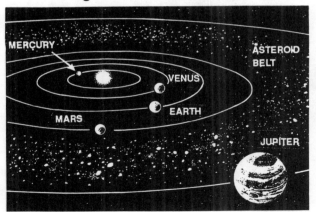

these rocks come? They are believed to be the remains of a full-sized planet that once existed between Mars and Jupiter, which either exploded or was torn apart by Jupiter's immense gravitational field. Astronomers have suggested that the ring of rocks may be the result of a collision involving a planetary body and another heavenly body in which both objects fragmented, and their remains are presently revolving around the sun in a fixed orbit.

Some 2,000 asteroids have now been catalogued in the asteroid belt. Some of the major ones have been measured. Ceres is 620 miles in diameter, Pallas — 334 miles, Juno — 150 miles, and Vesta — 330 miles. **(See fig. #52.)** Still others are mountain-sized chunks — tiny in comparison.

It is estimated that there are literally hundreds of millions of chunks around 10 meters in size that from time to time are affected by the immense gravitational influence of Jupiter. Many of them leave their orbit and begin traveling through space. In time, they will plunge into the surface of planets or moons like our own. Millions upon millions are yet to make an impact.

The two moons orbiting Mars are believed to be small asteroids which became trapped in its gravitational field. Both are under 10 miles in diameter. By the way, Mars, which is closer to the asteroid belt than Earth, has far more craters

Figure #52. CATALOGING THE ASTEROIDS

than the Earth's moon.

Rings Around the Planets.

There is a law involving heavenly bodies (such as planets) called Rochet's Limit. It states that if two large bodies are headed toward one another on a collision course, before they collide, the smaller body will be overcome by the gravity of the larger and will literally be torn into pieces.

(See fig. #53.) The pieces will then either plunge into the surface of the larger one or begin circling

Figure #53. ROCHET'S LIMIT

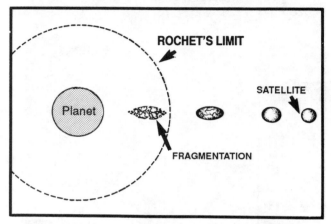

around the planet forming a ring. **(See fig. #54.)** It is believed that such is the case with Saturn, Jupiter, Neptune and Uranus, since all have rings of ice and stone circling around them. Fragments may even skip on the surface of the atmosphere of the remaining body back into space, much like a rock skips along the surface of water. They will find another target to strike later.

Back to Joshua 10.

Joshua 10 reveals that something happened in the heavens at that time causing disturbances from

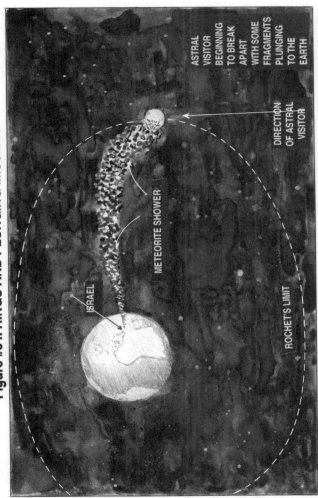

Figure #54. RINGS AND PLUNGING MISSILES

ASTRAL VISITOR BEGINNING TO BREAK APART WITH SOME FRAGMENTS PLUNGING TO THE EARTH

DIRECTION OF ASTRAL VISITOR

METEORITE SHOWER

ISRAEL

ROCHET'S LIMIT

above and below. Perhaps it was the fragments of some heavenly body coming to Earth in a shower of meteorites. Earthquake activity and meteorite showers can be attributed to the forces which govern the movement of heavenly bodies.[12]

The hailstones which bombarded Israel's enemy could have been fragments of another heavenly body which had ruptured into pieces. Or they could have been fragments from a ring of stones that circled a planet. As the planet drew near the Earth, perhaps fragments from its ring were drawn toward the Earth, plunging at blazing speed toward the ground as a shower of meteorites, pelting the army of the Amorites.

God was in control of every piece and fragment that fell. He caused the Amorites to be destroyed, but protected the Israelites from any fallout, just as He did when the plagues fell upon the Egyptians.

Not only can God use armies to bring judgment upon nations, He can use natural disasters — including comets, meteorites and even other planets — to cause catastrophic disturbances on the Earth.

Tektites.

Another possible explanation for the heavenly shower that pelted the Amorites is a deluge of stones known as tektites. Tektites are composed of natural glasses and have an unusual chemical composition which has become widely regarded as being of cosmic or of extra-earthly origin.

Scientists believe tektites were once liquid blobs which passed through the Earth's atmosphere at a high speed. The name is derived from the Greek word "tektos," meaning "molten." The stones are found worldwide, largely in non-volcanic regions, which signifies that they are not of volcanic origin. They come in many unusual shapes — resembling anything from buttons to barbells. **(See fig. #55.)**

Figure #55. TEKTITES: LIQUID BLOBS OF GLASS

Tektites did not fall individually; rather, they showered the Earth in great quantities. Discoveries in Australia and Southeast Asia reveal that at least 100 million tons of the stones pelted this area of the world at some time in the past. The largest piece found to date weighs in at almost seven pounds. Research reveals that tektites shatter into tiny fragments upon striking the ground. Thus the thousands of specimens which have been collected are considered to be pieces from larger tektite specimens believed to have been as much as one-and-a-half feet in diameter and to have weighed over 50 pounds.

Meteor Showers.

From time to time, Earth passes through a meteor stream which produces a meteor shower lasting from a few hours to a few days. A meteor stream is a collection of meteoroid particles left from the dusty path of a comet. The two most prominent showers presently occur each year around August 12 and December 14. They are quite spectacular to see, depending upon the observers' location, but do not present any threat of danger. However, in the past, such showers may have been far more threatening, as the fragments may have been larger. (See fig. #56.)

During Joshua's military campaign against

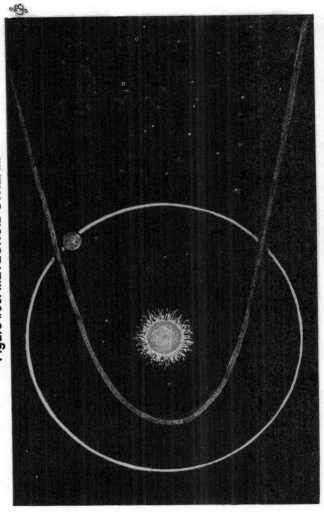

Figure #56. METEOROID STREAM

the Amorites, fiery rocks descended from heaven, killing more of the enemy than were killed by the Israelites (Josh. 10:11). No doubt, it was the same type of fiery death angel which killed 70,000 Israelites (II Sam. 24:15) in three days and 185,000 Assyrian soldiers overnight (II Ki. 19:35), as well as destroying the cities of Sodom and Gomorrah.

It is conceivable that in the past, a stray planet with a ring of meteorites came near to planet Earth. As it drew near, the Earth's gravitational field attracted fragments, which plunged toward the Earth at speeds of 20,000-50,000 mph.

Chapter Thirty

Exploding Heavenly Bombs and Other Biblical Catastrophes From Above

Siberia's Visitor From Outer Space.

On June 30, 1908 at about 7:15 a.m., something very large exploded in the sky over Siberia. It was not a nuclear test. Scientists believe that either an asteroid or a comet exploded about five miles above the remote Stony Tunguska River region of Siberia. **(See fig. #58.)** It ignited and flattened hundreds of square miles of forest. The explosion was heard for at least 600 miles. It destroyed an area equal to the cities of London and New York combined. The estimated strength of the blast was 1,000 times greater than the Hiroshima's atomic bomb blast of World War II.

This explosion that occurred in Russia's backyard may be a prototype from God to show this

Figure #57. THE GREAT SIBERIAN EXPLOSION

Figure #58. THE TUNGUSKA IMPACT AREA

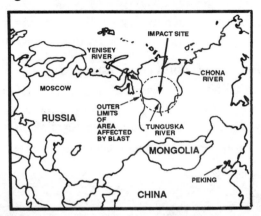

this generation the kind of destruction which will
happen once again on the Earth when the armies of
the North attempt to descend upon the country of
Israel. God's heavenly arsenal is capable of
destroying a massive land army in one mere blast.

> I will pour down torrents of rain,
> hailstones and burning sulfur on him
> and on his troops and on the many
> nations with him. ... I will send fire on
> Magog (Ezek. 38:22; 39:6).

There are numerous Scriptures which vividly
reveal that the Earth has undergone a series of
terrible and devastating catastrophes. Some of
these catastrophes were related to wars, others to

natural disasters, some of which are associated with heavenly events. The following examples suggest that judgment came from the heavens.

Sodom and Gomorrah Destroyed.

In Genesis 19, we read about the judgment that came upon the wicked and perverted cities of Sodom and Gomorrah. **(See fig. #59.)** Other

Figure #59. SODOM AND GOMORRAH

ancient records, such as the Talmud and the works of a Jewish historian, Josephus, record the destruction in graphic terminology. They heavily suggest that the catastrophe came from the sky in the form of exploding meteorites as well as hot volcanic debris.

Lot's Wife Turned to Stone.

Lot's wife, who Scripture reveals "became a pillar of salt" (Gen. 19:26), no doubt was entombed by ash, cinder and other falling hot debris from a catastrophe that originated in the heavens. Like the people of Pompeii (mentioned earlier), she became as a pillar or fossil of stone. In other words, she was fossilized after being covered with ash and other fallout material. Her body eventually turned from organic (living matter) to mineral (rock).

David's Disaster.

Disaster fell on King David's kingdom as a result of his attempt to take a census of his military troops.

The word "pestilence," used to describe the judgment on the nation of Israel (II Sam. 24:13 KJV), is again from the Hebrew word "deber." It is similar to "barad," and as previously mentioned, it might be better translated "meteorite matter." The judgment lasted for three days from Dan to Beersheba, taking the lives of 70,000.

This severe judgment came upon the nation of Israel, apparently because King David yielded to the temptation of counting his troops for the purpose of determining his strength — strength in numbers rather than trusting in the Lord as his strength and shield. God was displeased, and David and the whole nation of Israel paid dearly for his lack of trust.

The Assyrian Army.

Another biblical catastrophe occurred at the time of King Hezekiah. It is foretold and recorded in the book of Isaiah.

In Isaiah 10:12-19,34, God warns that He is going to punish the king of Assyria for his pride. The words in this passage relay catastrophic fiery destruction of his warriors and the land. Isaiah 29:6 prophecies that Israel would also be punished by the Lord. The verse mentions an earthquake, flames of devouring fire, tempest and wind. Isaiah 30:30,31 again foretells of the destruction of Assyria. The Hebrew word "shebet" in verse 31 is translated into English as "rod" in the New King James Version. Strong's Concordance says it comes from an unused root probably meaning "to branch off." It could easily mean meteors or meteorites — " branches" from a heavenly body.

God's judgment upon Assyria did come per-
haps in the form of an exploding meteorite.
Isaiah 37:36 tells us 185,000 men were killed.
The date of the destruction of the Assyrian king
Sennacherib's army is dated March 23, 687 B.C.
Amazingly, a Chinese document indicates that
on the same day, a catastrophe took place in
China: "Stars fell like rain, the earth shook, the
planets went out of their places in the sky."[13]

Disasters and Judgments.

There are many more catastrophic judgments
described in Scripture such as the Genesis Flood,
the destruction of the Tower of Babel, the
plagues that took place just prior to the Exodus,
the fall of Jericho's walls, and the sundial of Ahaz
incident. Each catastrophe seems to be
associated with heavenly events like that of
Joshua's Long Day.

No matter how these events took place, let one
truth be understood: The Bible clearly reveals
that wars and catastrophes come upon nations
because of their sin. Disasters are judgments.

The book of Jeremiah reveals that disaster
came to Israel because of its wickedness.
Through Jeremiah, God told the Israelites that if
they would return to the Lord, judgment could
be averted (Jer. 3:12-20; 4:1-4). But if there was

no repentance, an army from the north would soon be on its way to lay waste the cities of the wicked (Jer. 4:7). What would have befallen the ancient city of Nineveh had they not heeded the warning pronounced by the prophet Jonah, and repented of their sin? **(See fig. #60.)**

> The word of the LORD came to Jonah son of Amittai: "Go to the great city of Nineveh and preach against it, because its wickedness has come up before me." ... Jonah obeyed the word of the LORD and went to Nineveh. Now Nineveh was a very important city — a visit required three days. On the first day, Jonah started into the city. He proclaimed: "Forty more days and Nineveh will be overturned." The Ninevites believed God. They declared a fast, and all of them, from the greatest to the least, put on sackcloth. When the news reached the king of Nineveh, he rose from his throne, took off his royal robes, covered himself with sackcloth and sat down in the dust. Then he issued a proclamation in Nineveh: "By the decree of the king and his nobles: Do not let any man or beast, herd or flock,

Figure #60. AN OMINOUS OMEN IN THE HEAVENS

taste anything; do not let them eat or drink. But let man and beast be covered with sackcloth. Let everyone call urgently on God. Let them give up their evil ways and their violence" (Jon. 1:1,2;3:3-8).

Would Nineveh have had a cosmic catastrophe like Sodom and Gomorrah's had it failed to repent?

In recent decades, a nuclear holocaust has loomed over us. As terrible and awesome as that would be, nuclear power could not wreak nearly the destruction that the judgment of God could bring if He were to utilize the explosive power in the universe at His disposal on a wicked and perverted nation.

Throughout history, many nations have come to a sudden and destructive end. Some as a result of military campaigns, some by plagues, famines, droughts, earthquakes, tsunamis, volcanoes or other natural disasters. Still others, no doubt, have come to a sudden end as a direct result of destructive forces originating from the heavens. In the following section, we will examine additional documentation to confirm that the cause of Joshua's additional daylight time was associated with events occurring in the heavens.

SECTION V
HISTORICAL EVIDENCE

Chapter 31:   Additional Ancient
                    Documentation

Chapter 32:   Who Moved the Sun?

Chapter 33:   The Day the Sun Wandered
                    Crazily Across the Sky

Chapter 34:   "The Earth Reels Like a
                    Drunkard"

Chapter 35:   The Mysterious Retrogression
                    of the Shadow

Chapter 36:   The Greatest Miracle of
                    Joshua 10

Chapter 37:   Postscript Warning

Chapter Thirty-One

Additional Ancient Documentation

Parallel Accounts From the Ancients.

Today we Americans have a reminder of Joshua's Long Day. The early settlers in California named one of the desert plants the "Joshua tree." **(See fig. #61.)** Its shape reminded them of Joshua lifting his hands and commanding the sun to obey his words.

Most Christians are well aware of the biblical account of Joshua's command for the sun to stand still, but are unaware that there are similar accounts from many places around the world.

If Joshua's Long Day occurred as described in the previous chapters, the event would not have caused only a local disturbance, but would have been observed in many other parts of the world. This earthshaking event which occurred during Joshua's battle surely must have been recorded by the other nations of the world that

Figure #61. THE JOSHUA TREE

were affected by the heavenly visitor.

Are there additional records from other civilizations of a worldwide event at the time of Joshua? Yes, from every part of the world there are stories that have been handed down from the people living at that time. Long before the early American settlers named a plant in memory of Joshua's Long Day, there were numerous accounts left by the ancients as reminders.

The Book of Jashar.

In the biblical account of Joshua's Long Day, there is a reference to Joshua's prayer being in the *Book of Jashar* (Josh. 10:13).[14] According to tradition, this man was known as "Jashar, the Upright." His book is also mentioned in II Samuel 1:18. Jashar was a noted patriot who gathered songs and poems commemorating great events in Israel's history, as well as honoring its leaders.

The writer of Joshua calls attention to the fact that the miracle of the long day is preserved in the *Book of Jashar*. This historical document, which recorded the details of Joshua's military campaign, includes some information not mentioned in the Bible. For example, the division of time for the additional hours of sunlight is mentioned; however, the meaning of the phrase — "six and thirty moments"[15] or "six and thirty times" — has yet to be deciphered. No one knows for sure what measurement of time this represents. However, the fact that this book contains a record of Joshua's Long Day is additional historical evidence for the reality of the event.

There is a second biblical reference to the event in the book of Habakkuk. The prophet refers to the occurrence as an illustration of the wonderful power of a prayer-answering God.

> Sun and moon stood still in the heavens at the glint of your flying arrows, at the lightning of your flashing spear (Hab. 3:11).

The flying arrows and flashing spear no doubt refer to the hot meteoric material (hailstones) as mentioned in Chapter 27.

From Around the World. (See fig. #62.)

Amazingly, we find there are legends from every part of the world about a day in history when there was bewilderment over a deviation of the normal hours of daylight.

In the Americas, we find that the Aztecs, natives of Mexico, had a legend about the sun standing still for an entire day in the year of the "seven rabbits," which is the same time that Joshua was conquering Palestine. The Incas of

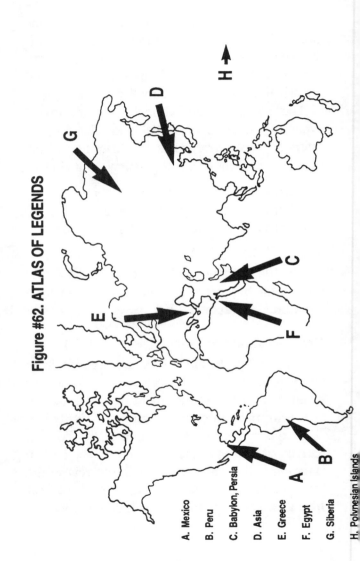

Figure #62. ATLAS OF LEGENDS

A. Mexico
B. Peru
C. Babylon, Persia
D. Asia
E. Greece
F. Egypt
G. Siberia
H. Polynesian Islands

Peru have a parallel account.

In the Middle East, the Babylonians and Persians have a legend of a day that was miraculously extended. From the continent of Asia, the ancient Chinese make reference to an extra-long day. Interestingly, their record states the event took place during the reign of Emperor Yeo, who was a contemporary of Joshua. One Chinese account reports that there was a "plague of vermin" and that "the entire land burned."

From the ancient Europeans, we have the Phaethon story recorded by the Greeks. And from as far east as Siberia the ancients wrote, "There was a sea of fire that fell on the earth." In Africa, according to the Greek historian Herodotus, the Egyptian priests had a record of a day that was twice the natural length. The Egyptian sage Puer wrote, "Gates, columns and walls are consumed by fire, the sky is in confusion, the fire almost exterminated mankind." Immanuel Velikovsky abundantly documents these reports of the ancients in his book, *Worlds in Collision.*[16]

The Polynesians have an amazing legend of an occurrence on the island of Maui in the Hawaiian Islands. This legend, called "The Snares of Maui," involves a day in the past when the sun was lassoed and immobilized for about a day.

Thread of Truth.

What is there to learn from these numerous strange and grossly exaggerated ancient traditions? They show a basic universal agreement that there was a day (or night) in Earth's history that was longer than normal, which confirms the biblical account of Joshua's Long Day. Although these ancient reports each include details that can be labeled as myth, there are similarities, a thread of truth, running throughout all of them.

Furthermore, these legends from various parts of the world indicate that disaster upon nations often came from the heavens. Many of these accounts mention fire raining down from above, which is similar to the biblical account of the hailstones (hot rocks) in Joshua 10.

For example, the Maya Indians of Central America report that rain, destruction and a sticky substance rained down from the sky with a great din of fire above their heads. A Quiche manuscript states there was, "a rain of bitumen from the sky." The *Annals From Cuauhtitlan* state, "Fire rain that fell," and it records a night that continued for an extended time (see Endnote #7, *Worlds in Collision*, pg. 67). Another report says, "The sky rained fire and red hot stones." From Brazil, it is recorded that, "the heavens burst and fragments fell down and killed everything and everybody."

Are these nothing but a collection of ancient myths about the gods who, from time to time, war with mortal man? Should we classify the story of Joshua in the same category as these reports? Or do we have a collection of historical documents which confirm the truth of Joshua's Long Day?

Legends of a Great Flood.

Many legends are believed to be about things which really did happen, although every detail in the story may not be true. And it is hard to believe that a similar story about an event occurring at the same time in Earth's history could have been made up by so many different peoples around the world.

For example, the story of the Great Flood has been found in over 200 accounts among people who could not have heard it from the Bible. The details of the accounts are not exactly the same as the biblical version; nevertheless, the numerous legends of a disastrous flood let us know there probably was one, even without taking into consideration the biblical account. The stories of a Long Day no doubt record a time in human history when the normal hours of a day were altered, showing that the biblical account is true and accurate.

Chapter Thirty-Two

Who Moved the Sun?

Karnak. (See fig. #63.)

There are some puzzling observations recorded by ancient astronomers, which seemingly can only be explained if the Earth's tilt has been dramatically altered. The mysteries involve the ancient calendars and the measurements of noonday shadows on the longest and shortest days of the year.

With today's technology, scientists are able to verify every ancient astronomical record. According to present-day calculations going backward in time, there is something wrong with these ancient measurements, though they were meticulously recorded. What makes the idea of error in these ancient measurements odd is the fact that the ancient astronomers saw a religious significance in their astronomical calculations and therefore took them very seriously.

The Egyptian Temple of the Sun (Amun-Re)

Figure #63. MONUMENT TO THE SUN-GOD

at Karnak (see fig. #64) in Southern Egypt (see fig. #65) is the site of a major religious ceremony that was held each year. It was known as the "Manifestation of Ra" — Ra being the Egyptian sun-god. Here, the pharaohs claimed to become divine when they became one with the sun-god, Ra, during the ceremony.

At the center of the temple was a darkened sanctuary filled with gold and other magnificently jeweled decorations. The sanctuary was connected to the outside by a long, narrow hallway. As the ancient summers drew near, the days grew longer and longer. The sun was positioned a little more northward each day, until it reached the most northerly point of its annual progression, marking the summer solstice and longest day of the year. (See fig. #66.) On that longest day, and only on that day, the sun set far enough north that it shined down the long corridor of Amun-Re and flooded the sanctuary with light.

Ra, Ra, Ra for Ra, the Egyptian Sun-God.

On that glorious day, the priests and other important persons would gather along the corridor, while the pharaoh stood in the darkened inner sanctuary. As the sun set, it shone down the long corridor, and the pharaoh was suddenly swallowed

Figure #64. EGYPTIAN TEMPLE OF THE SUN

Figure #65. BIRD'S-EYE VIEW

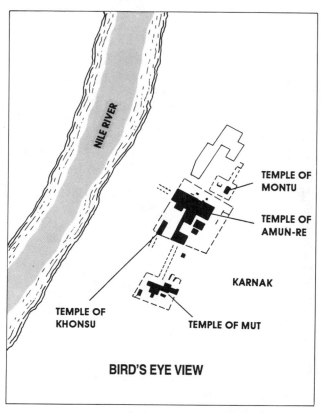

up in the blinding brilliance. **(See fig. #67.)** The sun-god, Ra, and the god, pharaoh, had become "one" — a most impressive ceremony, according to the records — except for one tiny problem.

Figure #66. MIGRATION OF THE SUN

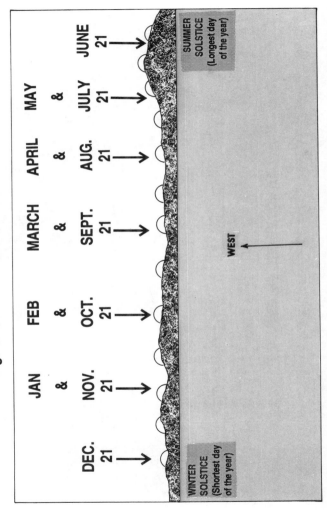

Figure #67. RA, RA, RA FOR RA

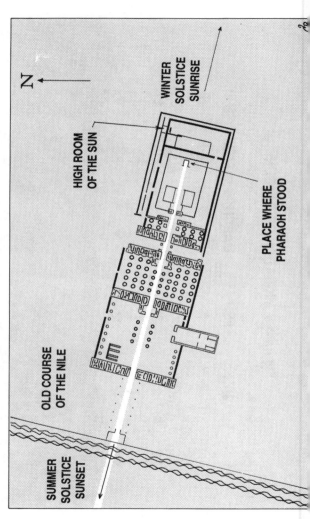

The Day Ra Failed to "Show Up."

According to modern astronomical calculations, during the time of the temple's historical use, the sun could not have reached far enough north to shine down the corridor and into the sanctuary. Yet we know from ancient hieroglyphic writings that the sun did indeed shine into the sanctuary on one day each year. Obviously, there is something wrong with or missing from our modern calculations. According to these calculations, it was at least 4000 B.C. when the "Manifestation of Ra" ceremonies were held. But according to biblical chronology, that's impossible.

Apparently, something dramatic has occurred in Earth's history to cause our globe to tilt, thus changing the position of the Earth so that the sun no longer sets at the same place on summer's longest day. Thus there came a day when Ra failed to shine down the long corridor and into the sanctuary. Apparently, Ra left on an extended vacation and never "showed up" again!

There are numerous examples of this same dilemma found around the world. The ancients constructed temples and structures in alignment with the winter and summer solstices, yet today, the sun does not rise or set in accordance with these ancient religious sites.

Stonehenge. (See fig. #68.)

One of the ancient sites which has mystified researchers is Stonehenge — an ancient man-made structure consisting of huge stone slabs arranged in circular patterns. It is situated on the Salisbury Plain in Southern England.

In ancient times, Stonehenge was used for astronomical observations in the context of religious rites and ceremonies. The difficulty that arises is once again associated with the measurements of the summer and winter solstice: They just do not line up with current astronomical measurements. Something catastrophic has transpired in Earth's history — since the construction of Stonehenge — which causes the calculations made today regarding the past to be out of sync.

Did the ancients simply miscalculate their measurements? Not likely. I have personally visited the Temple of the Sun at Karnak and Stonehenge. They both stagger the mind. It doesn't take a genius to recognize that to construct such temples was no small matter. It involved incredible mathematical and engineering skills equal to with modern-day technology.[17] No, the ancients did not miscalculate. There is another answer to why the sun does not line up with these ancient temples today.[18]

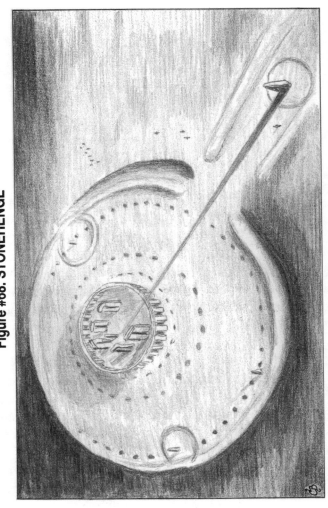

Figure #68. STONEHENGE

Chapter Thirty-Three

The Day the Sun Wandered Crazily Across the Sky

From the Polynesians.

Polynesia is comprised of scattered islands in the Central and South Pacific Oceans between New Zealand, Hawaii and Easter Island. The ancient Polynesians have a record in their traditions of a day when the normal hours were disrupted. However, instead of having additional daylight hours, they had additional hours of night.

Consider the tradition of the Maori of New Zealand. Their parallel account of Joshua's Long Day was that of a long night. Since Israel, where Joshua's battle occurred, is on the opposite side of the Earth from New Zealand, this would be expected.

What is amazing about the Maori account is that it tells that when the sun finally did rise in the sky, it "wandered crazily across the heavens."

In other words, it wobbled in its path across the heavens. **(See fig. #69.)**

As incredible as it may sound, there is tremendous significance to their statement that the sun "wandered crazily across the heavens." For it is likely that once the heavenly body had passed by Earth, the globe wobbled slightly as it slowly returned to a stable position, much like a spinning top does after it has been struck. **(See fig. #70.)**

Although this wasn't recorded in Joshua's account, it may have occurred as the Maori tradition states. Perhaps the Israelites, having had a truly "long day," were sound asleep. After all, when it was daytime for the Maori, it was nighttime for the Israelites. This Maori reference to the Earth's wobbling also helps to explain what is recorded regarding judgment in Isaiah 24:20: "The earth reels like a drunkard."

Figure #69. THE WANDERING SUN

Figure #70. THE WOBBLING EARTH

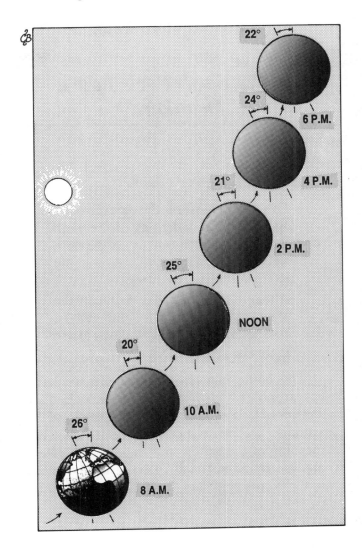

Chapter Thirty-Four

"The Earth Reels Like a Drunkard"

Isaiah's Amazing Perception.

> The floodgates of the heavens are
> opened, the foundations of the earth
> shake. The earth is broken up, the earth
> is split asunder, the earth is thoroughly
> shaken. The earth reels like a
> drunkard, it sways like a hut in the
> wind; so heavy upon it is the guilt of
> its rebellion that it falls — never to rise
> again (Isa. 24:18b-20).

The entire chapter of Isaiah 24 speaks of
catastrophic events occurring on planet Earth as
a result of God's judgment. In Chapter 28 of this
volume, we mentioned the significance and
meaning of the words "pit" and "snare," which
are also found in Isaiah 24 (vs. 18). In addition
to the words "pit" and "snare," we find another

significant phrase in verse 20: "The earth reels like a drunkard." This sheds light on the Maori's record that "the sun wandered crazily across the heavens."

What is Wobbling?

To the drunkard, the whole world, as well as the sun and the moon, is reeling. But it is actually the drunkard who is wobbling as he staggers along. An insect residing on the intoxicated individual would likewise see the entire world swaying.

Now, if the Earth were swaying, then those standing on the Earth would be swaying as well. Therefore, the ancient Maoris of New Zealand, on the morning after the long night, would have seen the sun moving across the heavens, seemingly in a wobbling fashion. However, in actuality it would not have been the sun that was wobbling, but the Earth on which they were standing. In fact, if the Earth were wobbling, all the objects in the sky — the moon, planets and the stars — would appear to wobble as they moved across the heavens. If a person had been able to observe the whole event from a spaceship a safe distance away, he or she would have seen that it was the Earth that was swaying like a reed in the wind, or as Isaiah states, "like a hut in the wind," rather than the sun.

Here we have a historical reference in Scripture in agreement with a tradition passed down by the ancient Maoris of New Zealand. Both suggest that the Earth has encountered disturbances which apparently affected its axis and orbit as it moved around the sun.

Consider a Spinning Top.

What would cause the Earth to wobble like a spinning top which has been bumped by an object? Let me illustrate to give you further understanding about Isaiah's incredible statement.

Picture in your mind a toy top spinning on the floor. What would happen to that spinning top if it were slightly bumped by some outside object such as a ball? **(See fig. #71.)** It would begin to wobble. The severity of its wobble would be determined by the severity of the impact.

The Earth spins like a giant top. Is it possible that on Joshua's Long Day, the spin of the Earth was disturbed by some outside force, causing the globe to sway and wobble? No doubt, this is exactly what happened. The effects were noted by the Maoris on the following morning when the sun finally rose on their side of the Earth.

Once the heavenly object passed, the tilt of the

Figure #71. TOPPLING A TOP

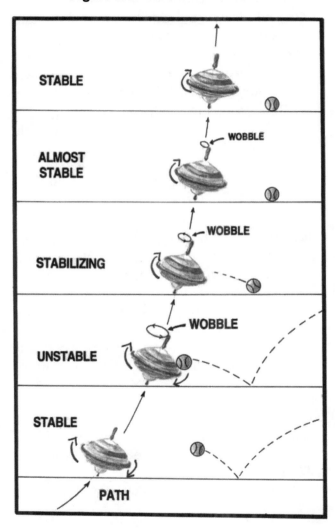

Earth would have resumed its normal (or its new) $23\frac{1}{2}°$ tilt — with a slight wobbling effect until it returned to its original stable condition as it continued its course around the sun. **(See fig. #72.)** It is possible that before this catastrophic event, the axis tilt may not have been $23\frac{1}{2}°$, but somewhat different. This would explain why the sun no longer lines up with the ancient temples, as mentioned in the previous chapter.

Why Isn't a Heavenly Body Mentioned in Scripture? (See fig. #73.)

If Joshua's Long Day was caused by a heavenly object passing close to the Earth, then why isn't there mention of it in the Bible? There is a possible solution to this puzzling question. Depending on where it passed the Earth, it may have been completely invisible to people on the Earth.

Consider our own moon. The new moon each month is invisible from man's viewpoint simply because its position is between the Earth and the sun. Occasionally, it passes directly between the sun and the Earth, which is known as a solar eclipse. Although we are not able to see it, we can see its effect on rare occasions. **(See fig. #74.)**

Likewise, the object which passed the Earth

Figure #72. WOBBLING THROUGH THE HEAVENS

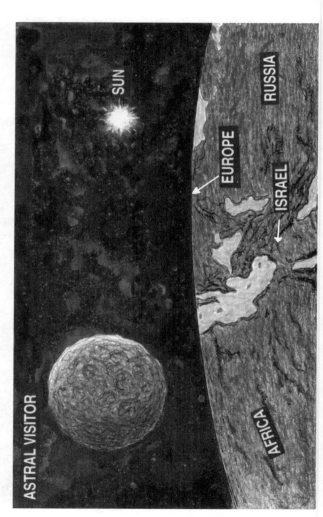

Figure #73. A HEAVENLY ENCOUNTER

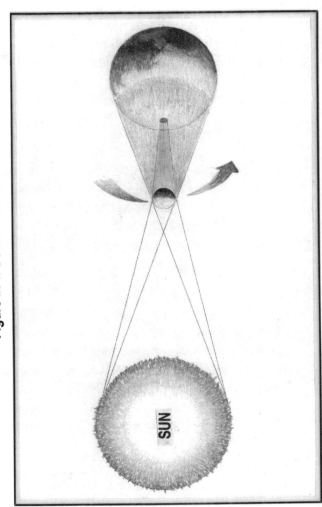

Figure #74. SOLAR ECLIPSE

SUN

in Joshua's time may have been shielded from the view of Earth's inhabitants. The ancients would not have noticed it because its appearance would have been like that of a new moon. In fact, since Joshua received more daylight, the Earth would have tilted toward the sun, suggesting that the heavenly body was passing between the Earth and the sun. This then would have resulted in the same effect as the new moon stage, when the moon is not visible from man's viewpoint on the Earth. **(See fig. #75.)** Then again, it could have been in a position totally out of view from where the Israelites were fighting. **(See fig. #76.)** Even something as simple as a cloudy sky could have shielded it from the Israelites' view.

Bucking Horses Which Carry the Sun.

Finally, it should be mentioned that on the opposite side of the Earth from the ancient Maoris of New Zealand and the same side of the Earth as Israel, comes the Greek myth known as the Phaethon story. This ancient account of the Long Day is particularly significant because it includes a similar aspect of the Maori account. It indicates the Earth was wobbling. A portion of the story reads as follows:

> The bucking steeds drawing the Solar chariot began bucking in the

Figure #75. THE INVISIBLE PLANET

Figure #76. OUT OF VIEW, OUT OF SIGHT

ISRAEL

Two possible locations of the heavenly visitor neither of which can be seen from Israel, even

morning.[19]

This portion of the ancient story is about the Greek sun-god, Helios, and his son, Phaethon. Phaethon wanted to drive the sun chariot for a day. Helios knew it would be difficult, but granted his son's request. The horses sensed Phaethon's lack of skill and veered off the heavenly path, bucking throughout the morning.

As fanciful as this ancient myth may sound, here we have another account of the sun wobbling as it moves through the heavens. And the story comes from a point in time that likely coincided with Joshua's event. Is this a mythological coincidence — or is it another corresponding testimony to the accuracy of the Bible's report?

Chapter Thirty-Five

The Mysterious Retrogression of the Shadow

"Behold, I will bring the shadow on the sundial, which has gone down with the sun on the sundial of Ahaz, ten degrees backward." So the sun returned ten degrees on the dial by which it had gone down (Isa. 38:8 NKJV).

Here is another reference to the Earth's axis fluctuating. Once again this is occurring along with other catastrophic events associated with phenomena in the heavens. Isaiah reports earthquakes, snares, pits, meteorite activity, the Earth reeling "like a drunkard," and the destruction of the Assyrian army.

Not only did the Earth's axis fluctuate during Joshua's battle, but it was also affected during the days of King Hezekiah when the Assyrians were advancing on Jerusalem to conquer it.

Hezekiah was sick, and he received a sign that he would recover. The sign God gave the king was that the shadow of the sun would move in reverse from its normal movement. In the days of the ancients, many cities had a sundial or obelisk **(see fig. #77)** by which one could tell the time by the advancing shadow upon it. **(See fig. #78.)** It was easy to tell the time as long as there was no cloud cover.

II Kings 19:35 tells us that it was during this time that "the angel of the Lord" killed 185,000 Assyrian men, destroying King Sennacherib's army. Remember that angel means messenger. Apparently, as in the days of Joshua, a hailstorm of meteorites associated with the passing of a heavenly visitor plunged down upon the Assyrian army, utterly destroying them.

A Lesson From a Toothpick.

To make a shadow retreat requires some variance of the physical mechanics governing the Earth's tilt and rotation. This can easily be demonstrated with a toothpick (or short pencil) representing the obelisk, a world globe representing the Earth, and a bright flashlight representing the sun.

Attach the toothpick to the globe over the

Figure #77. THE OBELISK: AN ANCIENT SUNDIAL

Figure #78. TRACKING THE SUN'S SHADOW

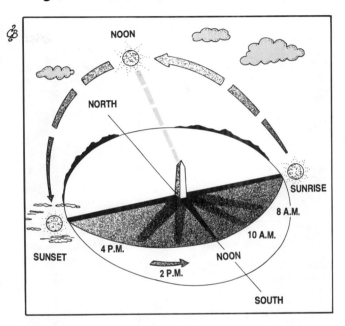

country of Israel. Point the flashlight toward the globe. Now, by maneuvering the axis tilt toward the source of light while rotating the globe you can see the shadow of the toothpick move in reverse from its normal motion. **(See fig. #79 A & B.)**

It is apparent that many of the catastrophic events recorded in the Old Testament occurred as a result of heavenly objects coming near to Earth. It seems there were many heavenly distur-

Figure #79A. REVERSING THE SUN'S SHADOW

TODAY

bances that menaced the Earth. Since the death and resurrection of Christ, we have been relatively free of such cosmic disturbances. However, the book of Revelation reveals that before the return of Christ, once again the heavens will become a source of catastrophic events occurring on planet Earth.

Figure #79B. REVERSING THE SUN'S SHADOW
HEZEKIAH'S DAY

Chapter Thirty-Six

The Greatest Miracle of Joshua 10

Why Would God Answer Such a Request?

The most important aspect of the passage in Joshua 10 is not the miracle of additional daylight hours. Rather, it has to do with God hearing and answering Joshua's request. Suppose you or I were to make such a plea. What do you think would be the chances of God responding? Probably less than zero. Why? Is it our lack of faith? No, I don't think so. In fact, Jesus pointed out that all we need is mustard seed faith to cast mountains into the sea. So a few more grains of mustard seed could easily move a heavenly object.

The reason Joshua found favor in God's eyes has to do with his response to a wilderness experience. Keep in mind that God said He would destroy the enemy. It was the Amorites' sin which made them ripe for judgment. They had been given numerous opportunities to turn from their wicked ways.

I believe the reason God answered Joshua's most unusual request was because of his trust in Him in the midst of the unbelief and skepticism of the Israelites some 40 years earlier. Joshua gave a positive report (Num. 14:6-9).

It is that same kind of unbelief and skepticism that is in the evolutionary camp today. Often we hear such statements from the evolutionists as: "God, why He could never do that in a million years." Yet, amazingly, the same mouths state that given an explosion and lots of time (billions of years), a universe can be produced.

A Bum Rap.

In spite of his positive faith, Joshua had to reap the consequences for the other spies' unbelief the same as the entire nation of Israel did. He took the "bum rap," wandering in the wilderness for 40 years before he could enter the Promised Land. Imagine the temptation to murmur and criticize God and his fellowman for receiving such an unjust sentence. Yet the record reveals that Joshua kept the faith and continually walked with God.

Eventually, God selected him to lead Israel into the land of giants. By that time, Joshua was around 80 years old. That is a good age to retire and forget about fighting any enemies, let alone giants.

"What Took You So Long, Joshua?"

Without hesitation, Joshua took up the challenge and proceeded into the Promised Land. Miracle after miracle followed him: the ceasing of the flow of the Jordan River, meeting the Commander in Chief of the Lord's army, the collapse of Jericho's walls, and victory after victory against well-trained and seasoned armies.

Then one day, he made what appeared in the natural to be a very foolish mistake. He made a ridiculous request of God in the form of a command: "Sun, stand still" (Josh. 10:12). Who in his right mind would have the nerve to do such a thing?

At this point, the Creator of the universe answered with a swift and emphatic "yes," as if to say, "Yeah! Yeah, that's My man. Joshua, what took you so long to make such a faith-filled request?" (DSV: Deep South Version)

The Heart of the Matter.

No doubt I have stretched the rules for biblical exegesis, but the heart of the matter is as follows:

By taking a closer look at the Hebrew words Joshua used, one can see that the reason for his request was to destroy God's enemies, not to get something for or draw attention to himself.

The Hebrew word Joshua spoke for "still" transliterated into English is "damam," which is found 21 times in Scripture. Everywhere else it is found it is translated "silent." It is only in Joshua 10 where it is translated "still."

The full significance of "stand still" is found in the word "stand" ("amad" in Hebrew), which is found hundreds of times in Scripture. God promised Joshua that he would be victorious over his enemies: "Not a man of them shall stand (amad) before you" (Josh. 10:8 NKJV).

Thus, to "be silent" meant the enemy (man or nature) would be powerless, and not able to gain the victory. Joshua was simply asking God for help to silence the enemies of God. And as a result, God used a part of His creation to destroy the enemy.

Stars Fight Against God's Enemies.

Occasionally, God uses heavenly bodies to defeat His enemies. With this in mind, another Scripture, which tells of a different battle that Israel fought some time later, may now take on new meaning.

> From the heavens the stars fought,
> from their courses they fought against
> Sisera (Judg. 5:20).

The Bottom Line: Searching Eyes.

> For the eyes of the LORD run to and
> fro throughout the whole earth, to
> show Himself strong on behalf of
> *those* whose heart *is* loyal to Him. In
> this you have done foolishly; therefore
> from now on you shall have wars (II
> Chron. 16:9 NKJV).

God is looking for opportunities to demon-
strate His power and strength through His
children. The problem is that His children are too
often busy asking for personal gifts and blessings
to build their own little kingdoms to ask for
things to help build the Kingdom of God. After
years of walking faithfully with the Lord, Joshua
made an unorthodox request from a natural
standpoint, and God responded favorably. The
fact that God answered this bold request is the
most incredible miracle of the passage involving
Joshua's Long Day.

Chapter Thirty-Seven

Postscript Warning

**Figure #80. SATAN'S TEMPTATION:
"DID GOD ...?"**

Why Bring God Into the Picture?

At this point, there is a temptation to wonder, since the laws of nature may have caused these events to transpire, why we should bring God into the picture. It could have happened without Him.

There are times in our lives when we need a

miracle. We cry out to the Lord and quickly receive the answer to our need. Afterward, we are tempted to disbelieve that God provided the answer and to believe that it might have happened anyway. Did God really do it? This is a tactic of the enemy. The nature of Satan, the thief, is "to steal and kill and destroy" (Jn. 10:10). He is deceptive and crafty. We must never give in to such seducing thoughts.

When we are tempted to deny God's intervention and believe the speedy answer to our need was only a coincidence, we must immediately reject the thoughts and give glory to God. We must always resist the temptation to think that a miraculous event could only have occurred through some natural process.

This is not a mind game of denial, but rather realizing that the enemy of our soul is a liar and a deceiver. The Apostle Paul reminds us that we must stand guard "that Satan might not outwit us. For we are not unaware of his schemes" (II Cor. 2:11).

We must constantly monitor the thoughts which pass through our minds. If Satan could deceive a third of the angels, then if we're not aware of his schemes, he can deceive us also. Satan deceived Adam and Eve with the question, "Did God really say ...?" (Gen. 3:1). And he has continued to use that same question to beguile believers throughout the centuries.

We must understand that God is in control of every atom in the universe He created, and He can guide any part of His creation to bring about His plans and purposes. The most difficult thing for Him to guide is a stubborn and rebellious heart. If we will allow Him, He can lead and guide us. If we will continue in rebellion, then He may even harden our hearts as He did with the pharaoh of Moses' day in order to accomplish His purposes and eternal plans (Ex. 7:3).

Conclusion

Christianity is a faith in the miraculous, beginning with Genesis 1 (the creation) to the incredible events of Revelation 22. God's Word doesn't tell us how miracles happen, it simply declares that God willed them to happen, and they did. God sometimes used His natural laws, but sometimes they were superceded by His supernatural laws as in the resurrection of Jesus.

The miracles of God rest, not on scientific analysis, but on testimony. While we can speculate as to how God may have accomlished miraculous events such as Joshua's Long Day, the bottom line is that God's children must accept them as true by faith. If God is powerful enough to create the entire universe, then Joshua's Long Day is but a minor incident. Those who struggle with this account no doubt have long since discarded God and His Word.

The Meaning of Joshua.

The name Joshua means, "The Lord is our salvation." How appropriate. For it is God's supernatural wisdom and power that is our salvation, not our own might or strength. May we sing with the psalmist:

> Some trust in chariots and some in horses, but we trust in the name of the LORD our God (Psa. 20:7).

Through the prophet Jeremiah, God reveals what He likes best in human beings:

> This is what the LORD says: "Let not the wise man boast of his wisdom or the strong man boast of his strength or the rich man boast of his riches, but let him who boasts boast about this: that he understands and knows me, that I am the LORD, who exercises kindness, justice and righteousness on earth, for in these I delight" (Jer. 9:23,24).

PART THREE
JONAH'S LONG NIGHT
SECTION VI
A WHALE OF A TALE

Chapter 38: Darts of Doubt
Chapter 39: Sounds a Little Fishy to Some
Chapter 40: Jonah II
Chapter 41: Here Am I, Lord, Send Someone Else
Chapter 42: The Jonah Principle: How to Miss God's Boat
Chapter 43: The Alien From the Sea: Jonah and the Fish God
Chapter 44: The Proof of Jonah's Authenticity
Chapter 45: The Greatest Miracle of Jonah
Chapter 46: Postscript: One More Lesson for Jonah

Figure #81. JONAH IN THE WHALE

Chapter Thirty-Eight

Darts of Doubt

Embellished Allegory?

The story of Jonah is one of the most ridiculed biblical accounts by so-called "intellectuals." So many critics have thrown darts of doubt through the centuries, a lot of people have a difficult time swallowing the idea that a whale could swallow a person whole, let alone stay in its belly for three days and survive.

Even some "Christian" theologians have suggested that the story of Jonah is nothing more than an embellished allegory meant to portray a spiritual truth about a man who strayed from God and how he returned. But, they say, the event never actually occurred.

Jonah: A Real Prophet and a Real Man.

It is obvious that people who make such accusations really do not know God nor His power. Furthermore, they do not understand that whenever a parable or an allegory is used in Scripture, it is evident in the context of the passage. The book of Jonah is written in such a way that it is easily understood to be an actual event in history. The mention of Jonah in II Kings 14:25 tells us that he was a prophet who lived in the Northern Kingdom about 825 B.C. None of the Jews or early Christians ever doubted the authenticity of the Jonah account.

Christ Himself not only referred to Jonah in His teaching, but shared the serious consequences of failing to heed Jonah's message of repentance. So to reject Jonah is to reject Jesus, accusing Him of ignorance, deception or lying.

The Denial of Miracles is Atheism.

It would be no problem for the God of Creation to prepare "a great fish to swallow Jonah" (Jon. 1:17), preserve him for "three days and three nights in the belly of a huge fish" (Matt. 12:40), and then to finally command the fish to vomit him onto dry land (Jon. 2:10). To deny that it is possible for God to accomplish a miracle is to deny the existence of God. This is atheism. One trusting saint stated it this way, "If God wanted, He could have provided a suite like that one at the acclaimed Waldorf Astoria Hotel in New York City with steam heat, Jacuzzi and even electric lights."

The skeptics' concern isn't really about the miracle of Jonah, but the existence of a miracle-working God. It isn't a question of Jonah's credibility, but God's ability.

Chapter Thirty-Nine

Sounds a Little Fishy to Some

Jonah's Suite: A Whopping Fish Tale.

What was the creature that swallowed Jonah? No one knows for sure, but the Hebrew and Greek words used in Scripture simply mean "a great aquatic animal." Before the rise of modern biology, the word "fish" in ancient languages applied to any sea creature. We can understand this, since today we use words as jellyfish, shellfish or starfish though none of these creatures are considered to be fish by modern biologists. Thus, in biblical times, "a great fish" could easily signify a whale.

It could have been a whale or a shark. In any case, the Bible says it was a fish that was specially "prepared" by God. There are several different species of whales, and even some sharks, that are quite capable of swallowing a man whole — without first chomping him into pieces. The sperm whale, the white whale and the whale shark can grow to be more than 70 feet long. **(See fig. #82.)** Each of these fish have been found with whole creatures as large as, or larger than, an adult man in their stomach.

All whales have storage chambers for air. In a large whale, the storage tank can measure up to 14 feet long by seven feet wide and seven feet high. This amounts to almost 700 cubic feet of space. This is enough space to take on a couple of seagoing passengers.

Also, there is always some air in a whale's stomach. And as long as the creature it has swallowed is still alive, digestive activity will not begin. Therefore, Jonah's experience could easily have happened within the framework of God's laws of creation. Yet it seems much more likely that the entire account involved a series of sovereign acts of God called miracles. Jonah's fish story was truly the all-time whale of a tale.

How Long Was Jonah in His Suite?

The length of time Jonah spent inside the fish could have been as short as 35-40 hours. This is because in the ancient Hebrew, "three days and three nights" was an idiomatic expression meaning the parts of three days.

In other words, the first day may have been only a few hours; the second day, of course, a full

Figure #82. GIANTS OF THE SEA

24 hours; and the third day may also have been only a few hours. Yet the time still would have covered three separate days of a week.

Even today, the "three day" expression is commonly used. For example, a conference may be advertised as lasting three days. Yet this may mean that it begins on the evening of the first day, continues through the second and ends at noon on the third. However, since God was looking after Jonah, he could have survived three weeks — or longer had God so desired!

A God-Appointed Fish.

One version of the Bible uses the word "appointed" when speaking of the great fish that swallowed Jonah. So God assigned a great creature of the sea for a particular purpose. He also selected a plant, a worm and a scorching east wind in the narrative. He didn't need to specially create these things, but directed His creation to fulfill a particular mission.

"Vomit, Fish!"

> And the LORD commanded the fish, and it vomited Jonah onto dry land (Jon. 2:10).

Sperm whales always eject the contents of

their stomachs when they are dying. The contents sometimes consist of huge masses equal to about six adult men.

"Come, fish. Go, fish. Vomit, fish." Does God know the language of fish? If we believe in a God Who created fish, then we must believe that He knows how to speak the language of fish, and that He called that fish to respond to Him.

If we can believe that God appointed the fish to swallow Jonah, then we can also believe that He called the ravens to feed Elijah. (See fig. #83.) We can believe that He closed the mouths of the lions when Daniel spent the evening with them, that He called the animals to come to Adam to be named, and that He called the creatures into the ark that Noah built.

It isn't difficult for a person to believe in miracles if he believes in God. But many refuse to believe there is a God. Why? Because God bothers them. He calls all people to leave their sinful, selfish ways and come to Him so that they might have eternal life. Man is the only creature who can refuse to obey His call. However, there will be an eternal price to pay for rebellion against Him.

Figure #83. ASSIGNED TO ASSIST ELIJAH

Figure #84. SWALLOWED BY A WHALE

Chapter Forty

Jonah II

Case Studies in History.

There have been a number of cases recorded in history where men have been swallowed whole by large sea creatures and were later rescued and actually survived. The Honolulu press reported a story of a fellow who didn't survive, yet was found in a giant shark without a broken bone. The headlines read, "Fishermen Find Body of Missing Merchant Inside Giant Shark."[20]

Some sharks have what is called the balaena, which is common to whales, in place of the teeth normal to sharks. So it cannot bite or chew, and must swallow whatever it takes into its mouth in one entire piece. The Rhinodon Typicus does on occasion swallow human beings — without harm to them in the process. The merchant who was swallowed whole was six feet long. There are additional documented reports of people surviving after being swallowed by a large fish.

The Story of James Bartley.

In February of 1891, a young English sailor named James Bartley was a crew member on the whaling ship, "Star of the East." It sailed the waters off the Falkland Islands in the South Atlantic, searching for whales. On one occasion, the sailors spotted a sperm whale. (When it was later caught, it measured 80 feet long and weighed 80 tons.)

Two boats with crew members and harpooners — one of them Bartley — were sent to kill the whale. As they closed in, one harpooner launched his eight-foot spear toward the creature. The instant it was struck, the whale twisted and lashed about. Its tail slammed into one rowboat and lifted it into the air, capsizing it. But the sailors soon subdued and killed the wounded mammal.

When the rowboat was righted, Bartley and another crewman were missing and written off as having drowned. The crew pulled the carcass of the whale alongside the "Star of the East" and worked until midnight removing the blubber. The next morning, using a tackle, the sailors hoisted the whale's stomach on deck.

According to Mr. M. de Parville, science

editor of the French magazine, *Journal Des De'bats*, who investigated the incident, movement was noticed in the whale's belly. When it was opened, Bartley was found unconscious. He was carried on deck and bathed in sea water. This revived him, but his mind was not clear, and he was confined to the captain's quarters for two weeks, behaving strangely and erratically.

Within four weeks, Bartley had fully recovered and related what it had been like to live in the belly of a whale. He remembered the whale's tail hitting his boat. Then, reported Mr. de Parville, Bartley was enveloped in darkness and felt himself slipping along a smooth passage. His hands felt something slimy all around him. The heat was unbearable, and he lost consciousness. When he awoke, he was in the captain's cabin.

For the rest of his life, Bartley's face, neck and hands remained white, bleached by the whale's gastric juices. Bartley stated that he didn't know how long he might have been able to live inside the whale because he had air to breath.[21]

Jonah and the London Museum.

The second documented account is about a man who was swallowed by a giant Rhinodon

Typicus, better known as a whale shark. The famous Jacques Cousteau and his boat, The Calypso, came upon one of these huge creatures, a 70-foot whale shark, on one of his expeditions in the Mediterranean Sea. The whale shark's teeth are not like those of the man-eating shark, but are more like a sieve. The size of these sharks is immense.

In the *Literary Digest,* there is an account of an English sailor who was swallowed by a giant Rhinodon in the English Channel. Forty-eight hours after the incident occurred, the fish was sighted and slain. The man was found inside — unconscious, but alive. When they docked at shore, he was rushed to a nearby hospital. He was only suffering from shock; otherwise he was in good condition. A few hours later, he was discharged having been declared physically fit. Not long after that, the man went on exhibit in the London museum. By paying a shilling for admittance, one could see the Jonah of the 20th century.

In 1926, the late Dr. Harry Rimmer, met this man in person and wrote about the encounter in his book, *The Harmony of Science and Scripture.* Dr. Rimmer stated that the man's appearance was a bit unusual: He was devoid of body hair, and patches of brown, yellow and white covered his entire body.[22]

There are other accounts of similar cases. There was an incident reported of a white shark swallowing an entire horse which had fallen overboard from a sailing vessel in the Mediterranean. In another case, a white shark swallowed a sea cow, which was the size of a lion.[23]

The miracle wasn't that Jonah was swallowed by a great fish, for we have evidence of similar cases today. The fact that Jonah survived for three days and nights inside the fish is amazing. Yet this isn't the greatest miracle recorded in the book of Jonah, as we shall see.

Today's news media carries story after miracle story of people who survive the most unbelievable circumstances. Yet people still disbelieve in God and give credit only to lady luck for such astounding occurrences.

The greatest miracle of Jonah has yet to be revealed. Meanwhile, let's search for a reason why Jonah didn't want to go to Nineveh.

Chapter Forty-One

Here Am I, Lord, Send Someone Else

Jonah's Hesitation Wasn't Peculiar.

By reading the headlines of the daily newspaper and watching the world news each evening, we can see that sin runs rampant in our world. The Earth is teeming with violence, anarchy, terrorism, rape and murder. Ruthless dictators reign in many nations. And in America, we continually hear about our overflowing prisons and serial killers on the loose.

In the U.S., there are more pornography outlets than there are McDonald's restaurants. Homosexuals, abortionists and drug pushers are everywhere. Murder, child abuse, fraud and corruption are common on the nightly local news broadcasts. Sometimes we wonder why God doesn't do something, and we find ourselves wishing for God's judgment to be released upon such wickedness. We think that surely these evildoers are beyond redemption. But other than wishing, what do we actually do to stem the tide of evil?

Nearly three thousand years ago, there was a similar reaction to evil in the land of Israel. The prophet Isaiah asked God why He didn't do something about the prevalence of wrongdoing in the land. Unbelievable as it may sound, God responded by saying in effect, "I can't believe that there is such terrible corruption in the land. Isaiah, why isn't anyone doing anything about it?" God was astonished that there was no one intervening on His behalf to thwart the wickedness (Isa. 59:16).

No, No, Lord! You Wouldn't Do That to Me, Would You?

Suppose in the midst of our thoughts, our wish for God's hand of judgment to strike a certain group of evildoers, God spoke to us to go and take the Gospel to them. How would we respond?

A modern-day example is the amazing story of Corrie ten Boom, who lost her family and friends in Hitler's brutal death camps during World War II. Although she managed to survive the horror, it was not easy for her to erase the memories of the atrocities she had witnessed.

Only her faith in God managed to keep her through it all.

Sometime after the war, after sharing her testimony at a conference, a German man approached her. She recognized him as one of the Nazi officers in charge of the killings in her concentration camp. He had since become a Christian, and with arms outstretched, he was asking her for forgiveness.

We can only imagine what must have flashed through her mind! She felt overwhelmed by the forces of hate and vengeance, but she cried out to God for help. An incredible power of compassion swept over her, and she embraced him, weeping and forgiving the man of the terror he had inflicted.

Jonah's Day of Opportunity.

Jonah, too, was faced with a formidable and loathsome task. Assyria was a great, but evil empire — a hated enemy of his people, the Israelites. **(See fig. #85.)** Nineveh was Assyria's capital **(see fig. #86)**. Its walls were about eight miles in circumference. Its size was a total of about 30 by 60 miles, much like one of our modern metropolitan cities with numerous suburbs surrounding it. The city was known for its treachery and cruelty toward its enemies.

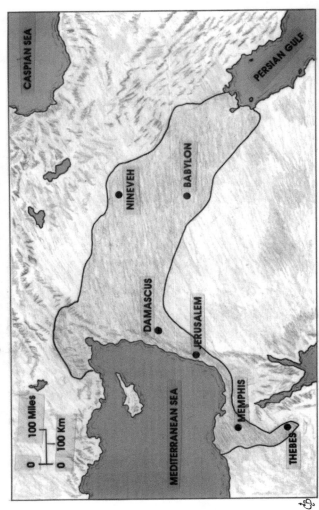

Figure #85. THE ASSYRIAN EMPIRE

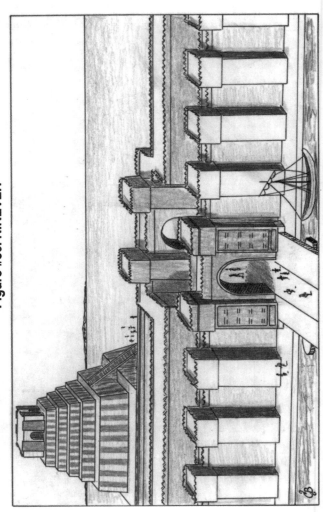

Figure #86. NINEVEH

The book of Nahum gives us additional insight about the wickedness of the Assyrian empire. It plotted evil against God (Nah. 1:9,11). It exploited the helpless and was cruel in war (Nah. 2:12). It was full of witchcraft (Nah. 3:4).

Now think about it. God had told Jonah to go to Nineveh and tell the people that He had seen their awful sin and that they were doomed. To Jonah, Nineveh was a brutal, merciless and anti-Semitic enemy of Israel. His going to Nineveh to warn the residents of impending judgment would be like an American Jew going to the city of Berlin in the time of Hitler's brutal dictatorship. "What, God? You want me to do what? Go and preach a message on the coming judgment? No thanks. Hawaii, here I come." It's not really hard to understand why Jonah ran in the opposite direction. **(See fig. #87.)**

God directed Jonah to go east to the great city of Nineveh and call the people to repentance. But fear struck Jonah's heart and he headed west for Spain — perhaps the Riviera. Pride may have also played a part in his decision to run from God's appointment. He may have been more concerned about his reputation than obeying God's Word, which is too often the case with ministers today.

Jonah knew that if the people of Nineveh did,

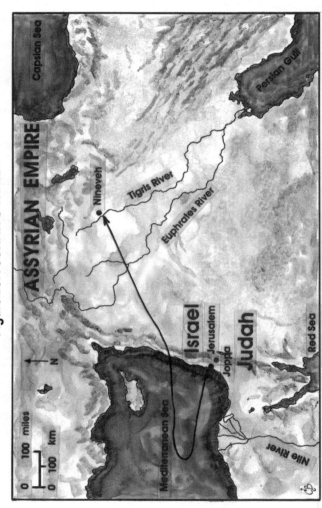

Figure #87. JONAH'S TRAIL

in fact, repent, none of his warnings of destruction would come to pass. This not only could be embarrassing, but could ruin his reputation and limit his invitations for future ministry. How often do selfish ambitions color our own decisions?

What Jonah feared came upon him. The people of Nineveh sincerely repented, and God took pity on them and did not carry out His plan to destroy them. Jonah became very upset and angry with God. God could have blasted Jonah for his defiant anger, but instead He ministered tenderly to him. In the final chapter of the book, we find that God taught Jonah a lesson about His compassion for the wicked lost — and His concern even for the animal kingdom.

Figure #88. MISSING GOD'S BOAT

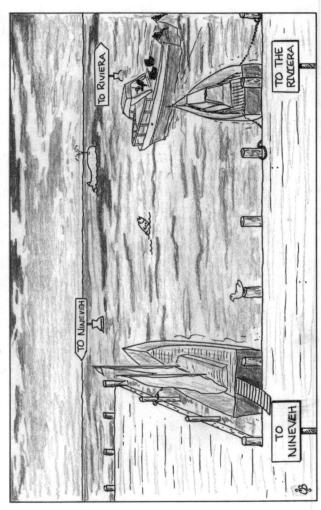

Chapter Forty-Two

The Jonah Principle: How to Miss God's Boat

"It Must Be God's Will."

Favorable circumstances are not necessarily conclusive proof that we are in the will of God. In fact, sometimes strong opposition can be an indication of God's will. But a callous heart can cause even the best of us to get on the wrong boat going in the wrong direction.

Steps to Missing God's Boat.

1. Jonah went the opposite way God clearly told him to go.

Note that when God said to go one way, Jonah went the opposite direction. Do some Christians today do that? God did not stop Jonah right away. Perhaps He was waiting for Jonah to think about his disobedience and decide to go to Nineveh after all. Remember, this is Almighty God, Who could have immediately halted the disobedient prophet.

2. Jonah found a vessel.

How convenient. Perhaps Jonah fooled himself into thinking God had changed His mind. After all, here was an open door — a wonderful opportunity. There will always be a means to carry us out of God's will. We don't have to look far. And Satan will be close by to assist us in our defiance against God.

3. Jonah had money for passage.

For some people, having enough funds to do something seems to be an indication that it is God's will. However, that is not always the case.

4. There was even available space on board.

One thing is for sure, there is always room on God's planet to walk out of His purpose and will. Some people look at every open door as though it came directly from the hand of God. But, as Jonah discovered, some open doors are not God-ordained.

5. Finally, Jonah was accepted aboard.

There will always be some people who will accept us when we are out of God's will. They may even encourage us in our disobedience. Acceptance by others, even Christians, does not mean we have God's stamp of approval.

No doubt, many of the ministers who have fallen in recent years were 20th-century Jonahs who were unwilling to yield to God's plan and purpose for their lives.

When All Else Fails, Pray.

It is both interesting and surprising that though Jonah was trapped in the belly of a large fish, it took him three days and nights to pray and seek the Lord. Even so, God responded to Jonah's prayer. It is never too late to pray. There are many Christians who, just like Jonah, know that they should stay in constant communion with God, and respond quickly to His voice. But they become lazy and calloused. Yet our wondrous God answers prayer whenever we get around to calling on Him. What an astounding God!

Jonah ran *from* God, and then he ran *to* God. Next, he ran *with* God — all the way to Nineveh. No doubt, he bore the scars from being in the fish, just as Christ did after He died and was in the belly of the earth for three days and nights. **(See fig. #89.)**

Figure #89. ABOUT FACE: JONAH'S FOOTPRINTS

Chapter Forty-Three

The Alien From the Sea: Jonah and the Fish God

What Led the People to Repent?

What led the people of Nineveh to repent? Was there something unusual about Jonah that made his message extraordinarily powerful? Remember the appearance of the two 20th-century men who survived their nightmare inside the belly of a whale? Their skin was abnormally affected by the gastric juices of the whale. One was bleached white and the other had patches of brown, yellow and white. Could Jonah's skin have looked extremely strange? Could Jonah have entered the city of Nineveh with a grotesque appearance and been viewed as an alien from the sea? Perhaps he shared his "too-much-to-swallow fish story," which would explain why Jonah's message caught the Ninevites' attention so quickly and so effectively.

Dagon: The Male Mermaid.

Archaeology has revealed that the people of Nineveh worshiped various gods, one of which was a fish god. According to some archaeologists, one of the fish gods of the ancient world was called Dagon. As a matter of fact, this god is mentioned several times in Scripture. It is made reference to once in the account of Samson.

> Now the rulers of the Philistines assembled to offer a great sacrifice to Dagon their god and to celebrate, saying, "Our god has delivered Samson, our enemy, into our hands" (Judg. 16:23).

And it was the statue of Dagon that kept falling down on its face until its head and arms broke off when the Philistines captured the Ark of the Covenant and placed it beside the god in its temple (I Sam. 5:1-7).

Statues and figurines of a god have been found in Nineveh by archaeologists. They are half-fish and half-human. **(See fig. #90.)** If Jonah arrived in Nineveh with a strangely repugnant appearance and an equally strange story of his adventure inside of a fish, he certainly would have captured their attention and been received

Figure #90. DAGON, THE FISH GOD

as a messenger from the spirit realm. Even the king was responsive to Jonah's message, and whatever he did, the people would follow.

The Sign of Jonah.

Jesus, in answering the religious leaders of His day when they asked Him for a sign to prove His claims, told them:

> None will be given ... except the sign of the prophet Jonah. For as Jonah was three days and three nights in the belly of a huge fish, so the Son of Man will be three days and three nights in the heart of the earth (Matt. 12:39,40).

Job 3:5 says, "Let the blackness of the day terrify it" (KJV). What was the sign of Jonah? Perhaps it was a disappearing act on the part of the sun — an eclipse — for three days and nights. According to Eugene Faulstich of Rossie, Iowa, Job 3:5 may be a reference to an eclipse of the sun. Solar eclipses were no doubt extremely frightening to the ancients, who attached supernatural significance to any unusual happenings in the sky. An eclipse of the sun must have terrified them, as this passage may be suggesting.

In a detailed study of Bible dates and history,

and with the aid of a computer, Eugene Faulstich believes he has discovered evidence that at the time Jonah preached to the people in Nineveh, there was a noon eclipse of the sun. He believes this added credibility to Jonah's message and that the people were so terrified, they repented. Whether or not Faulstich's research is accurate doesn't change anything. The amazing thing is, God knew how to get the Ninevites' attention.

A Sign From the Heavens.

As previously mentioned, the ancients were well aware that signs in the heavens had ominous significance. It is possible that at the very time Jonah was making his call to repentance, a heavenly object was approaching Earth and became visible in the sky. **(See fig. #91.)** Could the heavenly object have grown larger each day as it drew closer to the Earth during Jonah's 40-day prophetic warning? **(See fig. #92.)** Was God planning to bring destruction upon Nineveh via the heavens — as He did with Sodom and Gomorrah, the Amorites during Joshua's day, and the Assyrians during Hezekiah's time?

Figure #91. A SIGN IN THE HEAVENS

Figure #92. TRACKING THE HEAVENLY VISITOR

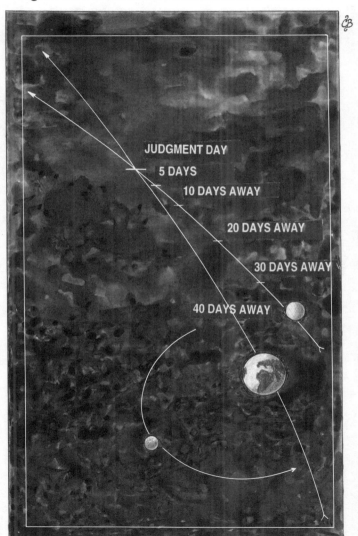

Chapter Forty-Four

The Proof of Jonah's Authenticity

Chasing Rabbits.

Chasing rabbits is useless, but some people seem bent on doing it anyway. One modern-day "rabbit" is the issue of Christ's burial clothes. **(See fig. #93.)** Over the years, there has been a lot of commotion about "the shroud." Movies have been made for and against the shroud's authenticity, causing questions and accusations to fly in all directions.

One thing is sure, the debate is a sign of our times. Christ pointed out that an evil and adulterous generation always seeks after a sign. He concluded by telling the disbelievers of His day that "none will be given it except the sign of Jonah" (Matt. 16:4). It seems it is human nature to get sidetracked and to begin chasing rabbits (signs), thus missing the "big game." **(See fig. #94.)** Jesus also said that "signs" will follow (not

Figure #93. THE SHROUD

precede) those who believe" (Mk. 16:17 NKJV).

The Proof is in Jonah's Pudding.

A person may think he has a good recipe for

Figure #94. CHASING RABBITS

pudding, but the proof of that is not revealed until the pudding is tasted. The Bible says, "Taste and see that the LORD is good" (Psa. 34:8). The proof of Jonah's recipe was not his effort in proclaiming his fantastic fish tale. Nor was the proof of his recipe demonstrated by an eclipse of the sun, a heavenly object looming in the sky, or his hairless skin in a rainbow of colors. Rather it was substantiated in the life-giving, transforming power of the words from God which he preached.

Likewise, Christ's rule in a person's life is not established by the discovery of relics such as Noah's Ark, the Ark of the Covenant, the shroud, etc. It is established by the Word of God, which will not fail to make the work of Jesus Christ evident even without all the proofs that man can discover to confirm it.

It is nice and to be expected that the physical world, which scientists investigate, does correspond with Scripture. But no physical evidence, be it for or against Jonah's fish or a supposed relic of Christ's life, can establish the saving work of God through Christ in human lives.

Christians are much better off concerning themselves with studying the Word of God than following discoveries of things like the shroud or the 20th century Jonah who was recently caught on video and shown on the television program, *911*. (A home video captured a fellow being swallowed up to his waist by a great white shark. And he lived to tell about it. He had the marks on his skull and body to prove it, even without the video.)[24]

Likewise, we would be better off concerning ourselves with the message of Jonah rather than the various side issues of the story. Chasing rabbits is fun for kids. But mature believers should be rooted in the Word of God and be a living testimony of the power of God's Word operating in and through them.

"Without Excuse."

Modern-day naturalistic skeptics who, in the face of overwhelming scientific and biblical evidence against evolutionism, still reject the fact of special creation, are "without excuse" (Rom. 1:20). Those who deny the fact of the cataclysmic destruction that came upon the Amorites during Joshua's Long Day, despite the great body of evidence supporting it, are "willingly ... ignorant" (II Pet. 3:5 KJV). Those who reject the "sign of Jonah" will not, according to Jesus, receive another: "A wicked and adulterous generation looks for a miraculous sign, but none will be given it except the sign of Jonah" (Matt. 16:4).

Jesus referred to the account of Jonah and used it as a "sign" of His own impending death and resurrection, which would be the sign confirming His deity and the significance of His work on Earth so that man might be saved. Jonah's experience in the whale prophesied the duration of Christ's time in the grave (three days and three nights).

The most varied and abundant evidence of any event in ancient history is available in support of the fact of Christ's bodily resurrection. Yet, He said: "If they do not listen to Moses and the Prophets, they will not be convinced even if someone rises from the dead" (Lk. 16:31).

It is sad, but true, that most modern intellectuals continue to deny the Creator, explain away Joshua's Long Day, and ridicule Jonah's fish story — not to mention ignoring the irrefutable evidence of Christ's resurrection. They continue to reject the infallible Word of God and refuse His offer of forgiveness and eternal life through Christ and so will die in their sins.

They will be "without excuse" when they stand before God and are called to account for crushing the truth and "deliberately" forgetting the Creator (Rom. 1:20; II Pet. 3:5). The rocks of the Earth will testify against them (Lk. 3:8;

19:40). Yes, even the rocks of the past like those that fell upon the Amorites during Joshua's Long Day and those of the fiery judgment to come. The converted Ninevites who believed and accepted the message of Jonah will bear witness against all those who refuse to believe in the One greater than Jonah.

Objections can always be raised to the most persuasive Christian evidences, but the Scriptures warn that such an attitude is dangerous folly. "The fear of the LORD is the beginning of knowledge, but fools despise wisdom and discipline" (Prov. 1:7).

In the meantime, Christians have abundant "reason for the hope that they have" (I Pet. 3:15). Though now, it must remain hope (not "seen," as noted in Romans 8:24) until Christ returns.

Chapter Forty-Five

The Greatest Miracle of Jonah

The Miracle and the Message of the Book of Jonah.

The greatest miracle of Jonah isn't that a great fish of the ocean swallowed him, nor that he survived three days and nights in its belly. Skeptics would have us overlook the most amazing aspect of the story of Jonah. The miracle of the book is that over half a million people were saved. The miracle was that the message of hope and forgiveness was received and believed.

The book of Jonah is not about a great fish, but a great and merciful God. It is a story of a reluctant missionary who took the Gospel to a pagan nation. The fish incident was superfluous. The miracle was that about 600,000 people came to know the Lord. What a successful evangelistic crusade!

The miracle of the book of Jonah is that the people of Nineveh were saved. The message is that our God is full of mercy and grace. No one deserved His forgiveness less than the people of Nineveh.

The issue at this point is what are we going to do with the message of God's love and grace? How are we going to respond to it? No doubt, some of you reading this book have never personally received Christ Jesus into your heart. If God can deliver a man from a fish, then He is able to change hearts. He is able to give life and light, and the hope of spending eternity with Him. He is asking you for a positive response. Ask Christ Jesus to become your Savior. More important than knowing the truth about Jonah's episode with a fish is knowing the truth of His message. The message of Jonah is still relevant today.

> In the past God overlooked such ignorance, but now he commands all people everywhere to repent. For he has set a day when he will judge the world with justice by the man he has appointed. He has given proof of this to all men by raising him from the dead (Acts 17:30,31).

Chapter Forty-Six

Postscript: One More Lesson for Jonah

Jonah Sulks.

Once Jonah finished his mission (Jon. 4), God had to confront him again. It seems that he had preached God's message out of duty rather than compassion. So after Nineveh repented, Jonah sulked. He was angry that God had changed His mind about sending judgment upon Nineveh. He didn't think those people deserved God's mercy, even though they had repented of their wickedness. God confronted Jonah about his self-centeredness and lack of compassion. Jonah had forgotten the original purpose of Israel as a nation: to be a blessing to the world by sharing God's message of love with other nations.

> Through your (Abraham's) offspring all nations on earth will be blessed, because you have obeyed me (Gen. 22:18).

Figure #95. GOD LOVES CHILDREN — AND ANIMALS, TOO

Are we like Jonah when we hear about some unlikely person who turns to God and repents? Maybe we have a narrow view like Jonah. Even Christ's own disciples didn't want to share God's message with Gentile nations. Yet God's love and mercy are available to all who come to Him today in faith.

God Loves Cows, Too.

Not only do we read that God was concerned about the people in Nineveh, but His compassion reached to the animals, too.

> Nineveh has more than a hundred and twenty thousand people who cannot tell their right hand from their left, and many cattle as well. Should I not be concerned about that great city? (Jon. 4:11).

Jonah was aware of God's incredible compassion for mankind, but he was not willing to pattern himself after God's example.

> I knew that you are a gracious and compassionate God, slow to anger and abounding in love, a God who relents from sending calamity (Jon. 4:2).

When we see the full picture of the God of the

universe and His love and compassion for even the most rebellious of His creatures, we can only fall on our faces and ask for forgiveness. The Gospel is for all who will repent and believe. No one is beyond redemption.

Yet, hearing the Word of God is not enough. Responding to it is what brings salvation. God forgave Nineveh's sinfulness, just as He had forgiven Jonah's rebellion. The purpose of God's judgment is correction, not revenge. He is always ready to show compassion to anyone willing to seek Him.

PART IV
JOSHUA AND JONAH'S
PROPHETIC SIGNIFICANCE

SECTION VII
THE GODS OF CATACLYSM

Chapter 47: Ancient Mythology and Astral Catastrophism

Chapter 48: Worldviews of the Ancients

Chapter 49: The Origins of Astrology

Chapter 50: The Abominations of the Pagans

Chapter 51: The Gods of the Greeks

Chapter 52: The Gods on Our Calendars

Chapter 53: Halloween and Friday the 13th

Chapter 54: Cosmic Warfare and Hairy Comets

Chapter 55: What if We Had Been Alive in Those Days?

Chapter Forty-Seven

Ancient Mythology and Astral Catastrophism

Looking Into the Past Towards the Future.

The stories of Joshua and Jonah are truly remarkable accounts of God's miraculous intervention in the lives of two individuals. The realization that the physical heavens were involved brings to light some amazing revelations within Scripture.

At this point, we could conclude this volume. However, it seems that it would be beneficial to the reader to share some additional corresponding and intriguing aspects about the ancient civilizations that can give us tremendous insight into events told about in Scripture, both past and future. We shall, therefore, continue our study of the gods of cataclysm and conclude with the God of Revelation and the coming holocaust prophesied in the book of Revelation.

Have You Ever Wondered Why?

Have you ever wondered why Greek mythology contains so much cosmic warfare involving the planetary gods? Did you know that the seven days of our week are named after the five visible planets and the sun and moon? Even several of the months of the year have been named after the visible planets. History reveals that these cosmological deities (planet gods) were worshiped from 2000 B.C. to 500 B.C., and that planet worship was widespread throughout the world.

Our present calendar has $365\frac{1}{4}$ days in a year, but the ancient calendar only consisted of 360 days. No one knows for sure what happened, but the calendar may have changed due to an orbital shift caused by another heavenly body's gravitational field interacting with the Earth's as it passed by. Thus our globe may have been disturbed or even bumped out of its original orbit into the present one that requires an additional five and a quarter days.

As previously mentioned, the effects on the Earth would have been catastrophic if an astral visitor came near our planet in the past. That would certainly explain why so many ancients around the world paid so much attention to the movement of the planets and cometary visitors. Some astral occurrences or visitors may have been cyclical, bringing catastrophes or threats of such at expected times, once calculations were made.

If all of this sounds like something out of a science fiction movie, it is because evolutionism has taught for decades that there is no God or supernatural realm — that religion is nothing more than a superstition concocted by primitive man because he could not understand his surroundings. The truth of the matter is that evolutionism is the myth, and the ancients had far greater insight into the supernatural than for what we give them credit.

Astral Catastrophism.

Catastrophism associated with the heavens is related to celestial phenomena, which was and is still under the direct sovereign control of God's hand. On occasion, He has used the heavens to bring judgment upon wicked nations. Under such circumstances, it is not difficult to understand why many of the ancients prayed to and worshiped celestial bodies as well as charted their movements to see when they might expect future catastrophes.

For example, the calendar of the Maya Indians of Central America related the position of the planets 3,000 years in the future or in the past — to the thousandth decimal point. Such dedication to precision is almost beyond explanation, unless we understand the ancients' experience with cosmic catastrophies and concern regarding future ones.

The idea of astral catastophism correlates well with historical records, geophysical evidences and scientific principles, as well as with the Bible. Within this system of thought, it should be no surprise that ancient architectures, calendars, religious themes, and even military campaigns were all centered around planetary movements, eclipses, zodiacs, astrologies and other astronomy-related phenomena.

Realizing the ancients lived under constant threat of cosmic catastrophes, it is easier to understand why so many civilizations of the past worshiped the planets and carefully measured their paths in the sky. They mapped the zodiac in which they moved and looked heavenward in panic and fear. Yet sometimes, they also looked with hope — that their enemies would be consumed by a catastrophe from the heavens.

Figure #96. GODS OF CATACLYSM

Chapter Forty-Eight

Worldviews of the Ancients

Mythological Records?

Upon realizing that there are numerous passages within Scripture confirming that disasters which fell upon nations often came from the heavens, it would be advantageous to look more in depth at the traditions of the ancients. This will give us insight into the prophetic significance of Joshua and Jonah and other biblical catastrophes of the past, as well as those predicted for the future in the book of Revelation.

The ancients believed gods of the heavens actually fought one another and hurled lightning bolts at anyone who offended them. Why is it that so much of ancient mythology contains stories of planetary gods who are constantly involved in cosmic warfare and causing havoc to the mortals on planet Earth? (See fig. #96.) Is it possible that they were closer to the truth than we have realized?

Read the words of King David as he declares how his Lord delivered him from the hands of his enemies:

> The earth trembled and quaked, the foundations of the heavens shook; they trembled because he was angry. Smoke rose from his nostrils; consuming fire came from his mouth, burning coals blazed out of it. He parted the heavens and came down; dark clouds were under his feet. He mounted the cherubim and flew; he soared on the wings of the wind. He made darkness his canopy around him — the dark rain clouds of the sky. Out of the brightness of his presence bolts of lightning blazed forth. The LORD thundered from heaven; the voice of the Most High resounded. He shot arrows and scattered the enemies, bolts of lightning and routed them. The valleys of the sea were exposed and the foundations of the earth laid bare at the rebuke of the LORD, at the blast of breath from his nostrils (II Sam. 22:8-16).

Taking astral catastrophism into consideration, the ancients' worship of astral entities astral entities doesn't sound quite so ridiculous, does it? At least it was logical, once we understand their perspective and its basis. The myth of evolutionism is far more absurd. So which contains the real 20th-century science fiction — evolutionism or the Bible?

Celestial Concerns.

Many of the ancient records describing cataclysms have been classified as mythology by the intellectual community. Some of these cataclysmic events have been the object of much research. A common thread that runs through many of the traditions of the ancients is that they were preoccupied with the heavens and the celestial bodies. It is obvious that theirs was not a casual interest simply for recreation; rather, they were obsessed by the subject, and it permeated every part of their societies.

Many of the ancient wise men believed that the Earth experienced periodic worldwide disasters which dramatically altered its face, and in some cases, annihilated life. Ancient records and archaeology reveal that people from every corner of the globe were convinced that catastrophes were associated with the heavens. They believed that many of the upheavals on the Earth had been accompanied by irregularities in the heavens. Thus they tracked celestial bodies with great concern and apprehension in anticipation of further disturbances.

Obelisks, ziggurats, sundials, pyramids and similar structures could be found everywhere throughout the ancient world. They were constructed to trace the paths and movements of the sun, moon, planets, comets, stars and the associated heavenly phenomena. Today, most of these structures have been classified as relating to mythology.

Of course, these objects do contain some imaginative accessories, but they also contain much truth. When did the ancients begin their quest to chart the skies and construct temples in honor of heavenly deities? It began shortly after Noah's Flood.

Chapter Forty-Nine

The Origins of Astrology

Shortly After the Flood.

Historical documents collected from various civilizations around the world reveal that after the Flood (around 2500 B.C.), from the time the Tower of Babel was built around 2000 B.C. until about 700 B.C., the heavens were in a state of cosmic disturbance. In other words, ancient documents reveal that the celestial bodies were involved in some sort of cosmic relationship with the Earth. From time to time, there were disturbances in the heavens which brought destruction to the Earth.

The relationship of at least some of these heavenly bodies with Earth may have been predictable because their orbits were observable. That's why many of the ancients began worshiping these heavenly intruders. This worship led to thousands of temples dedicated to the gods of the heavens being constructed around the world. **(See fig. #97 A&B.)**

Figure #97A. ASCENDING TO THE HEAVENS

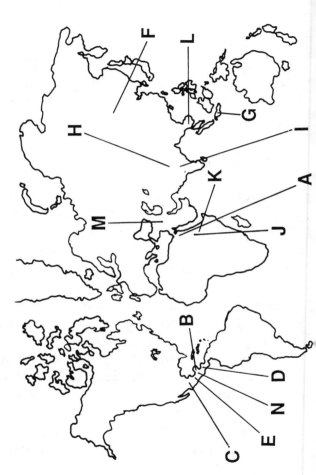

Figure #97B. ASCENDING TO THE HEAVENS

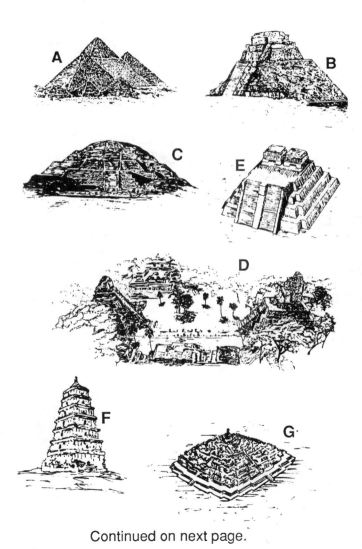

Continued on next page.

The Origin of Planetary Deities.

It was after the Flood that mankind suddenly developed an intense and passionate interest in planetary movements — eclipses, zodiacs, astrologies and other astronomy-related phenomena. People were focused on the wrath of planetary deities, even to the point of worshiping the planets, the sun and the moon. This was true with the Babylonians, Egyptians, Phoenicians, Orientals, Romans, Greeks, Europeans, Aztecs, Mayas — and even the Hebrews. God speaks about the kings and officials of the Jews:

> At that time, declares the LORD, the bones of the kings and officials of Judah, the bones of the priests and prophets, and the bones of the people of Jerusalem will be removed from their graves. They will be exposed to the sun and the moon and all the stars of the heavens, which they have loved and served and which they have followed and consulted and worshiped (Jer. 8:1,2).

Abraham and Job.

It is believed that Abraham and Job lived during the same time, which was about 10-12 generations after the Flood. This was an era when worship of the sun, moon and the "hosts of heaven" (planetary deities and other sky gods) was becoming world-wide. Job objected forcefully:

> If I have regarded the sun in its radiance or the moon moving in splendor, so that my heart was secretly enticed and my hand offered them a kiss of homage, then these also would be sins to be judged, for I would have been unfaithful to God on high. (Job 31:26-28).

Abraham left the Ur of the Chaldees, which was becoming engulfed in astrology, complete with astronomer-priests and temple towers known as ziggurats.

The Construction of Temple Towers.

Archaeological evidence reveals that it was shortly after the Flood that the peoples of the world began constructing temples dedicated to the sun and planets. They constructed obelisks and gnomons which not only indicated the times and the seasons, but became objects of worship.

The first building of a tower recorded in Scripture was that of the Tower of Babel. It is said to have had a construction force of 600,000 slaves. **(See fig. #98.)**

Figure #98. THE TOWER OF BABEL

The ancient Mayas and Aztecs erected hundreds of pyramid towers throughout Central America. And then there are the magnificent pyramids of Egypt **(see fig. #99)**, which in the language of the Egyptians, means "reaching or ascending into the heavens." In Great Britain alone, over 500 astronomical temples have been discovered dating between 1900 B.C. and 1600 B.C. The most famous was Stonehenge. Something in the heavens had caught the attention of

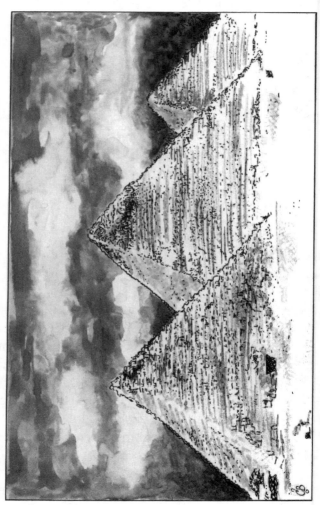

Figure #99. THE TOWERING TEMPLES OF TIME

the peoples around the world.

It wasn't until around 700 B.C. that from historical evidence we find that the heavens settled down for the most part, and astronomical peace came to planet Earth.

Contempt and Scorn From Evolutionists.

This view of astral catastrophism is reflected in and supported by the histories of the ancients as well as the Bible. Yet evolutionists laugh and scorn at such a concept as though it were a mere fable. However, it must be understood that evolutionists consider the entire Bible as mere fiction. They do not want to consider, let alone accept, anything that brings a Creator God into the picture — and especially God Who, through His Son and His Word, would expose their sin for all to see.

There are even some evangelical Christians who find it difficult to accept such ideas and concepts. This is the result of evolutionary dogmas of uniformitarianism having been forced onto the public as unquestionable truth over the last century. Lack of acceptance of astral catastrophism on the part of an evangelical Christian could also reflect a lack of knowing and seeing the power of God in his own personal Christian experience.

Chapter Fifty

The Abominations of the Pagans

Appeasing the Gods.

Is it any wonder that so many of the ancient civilizations practiced human sacrifice? Their fear drove them to their abominable practices involving the sacrificing of babies, virgins and other victims by the thousands. It also drove them to commit other atrocities. That explains why some nations came to a sudden end. They were either destroyed by some cataclysmic event or by an invading army — acts of judgment on evil from the hand of God.

Our modern intellectual community tends to dismiss all ancient religious rituals as practices of ignorant people with no basis in fact. This is because evolutionary atheistic humanists deny the reality of the spiritual world. Consequently, anything sounding like supernatural judgment coming out of heaven, such as the biblical story of the destruction of Sodom and Gomorrah, is ridiculed as unrealistic mythology.

Human sacrifice became widespread around the world in hopes of appeasing the gods of the heavens so that destruction might be averted. The evil practices in which the nations involved themselves to try to keep the gods from raining fire and brimstone down upon them incurred God's righteous anger and forced Him to bring judgment upon them.

Consider the difference in God's treatment of the Hebrews and the Egyptians at the Passover just prior to the Exodus. The sacrifices God required of the Hebrews didn't involve humans, but animals. However, because of the pharaoh's stubborn resistance to Moses' pleas to let the Hebrews go, the firstborn Egyptian children died at God's hand. Even after watching that dreadful event, and no doubt being aware that the Egyptians' worship of the false gods contributed to God's wrath, Israel eventually followed suit.

The Hebrews Followed Suit.

Not only did the pagans involve themselves in such practices; the Jewish people, likewise from time to time, worshiped the false gods of the heavens. Scripture reveals that some of Israel's kings led the nation into idolatry. For instance, Manasseh was a very evil king. He began to consort with the priests and priestesses of Baal and became apostate. We are told that he worshiped all the hosts of heaven and even sacrificed his own son to them.

> He did evil in the eyes of the LORD, following the detestable practices of the nations the LORD had driven out before the Israelites. He rebuilt the high places his father Hezekiah had destroyed; he also erected altars to Baal and made an Asherah pole, as Ahab king of Israel had done. He bowed down to all the starry hosts and worshiped them. ... In both courts of the temple of the LORD, he built altars to all the starry hosts. He sacrificed his own son in the fire, practiced sorcery and divination, and consulted mediums and spiritists. He did much evil in the eyes of the LORD, provoking him to anger. He took the carved Asherah pole he had made and put it in the temple (II Ki. 21:2,3,5-7).

Chapter Fifty-One

The Gods of the Greeks

Superstitious Tales?

Almost everyone is familiar with Greek mythology and the traditional humanistic view that it is nothing more than a group of pagan legends of fantasy and fiction. Hollywood produces motion pictures that reinforce modern man's opinions that these ancient legends are imaginary myths. However, there is more fact to many of these myths than we might suppose.

Many of the well-known gods of Greek mythology are associated with astral catastrophism. The names of some of these mythological gods are: Ares or Aphrodite — god of Mars; Zeus — god of Jupiter; Apollo — originally god of Mars, later the sun; Hermes — god of Mercury; Cronus — god of Saturn; and Poseidon — god of earthquakes and tidal waves. **(See fig. #100.)**

These gods were worshiped by the ancients, and there are thousands of traditions, legends and

Figure #100. CLASSICAL GODS OF THE GREEKS

A

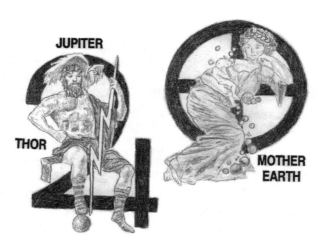

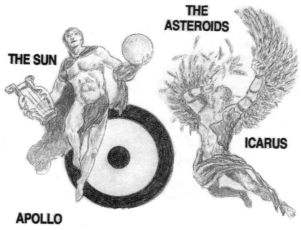

Figure #100. CLASSICAL GODS OF THE GREEKS

B

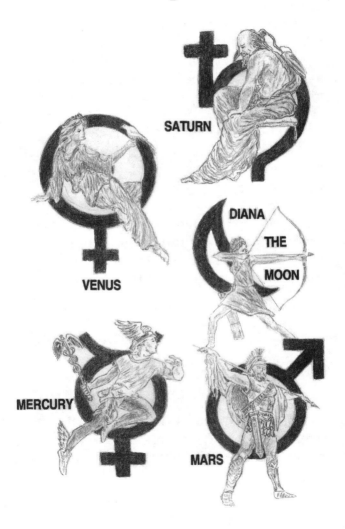

tales about these deities. It is incredible that so many manuscripts have survived, since they are considered nothing more than superstitious tales by the humanistic community of our day. But remember, they also consider Noah's Flood a myth, even though several hundred accounts of a global flood have been collected from various tribes, races and cultures from around the world.

The Hebrews.

Although the pagans believed the planets themselves were gods, the Hebrews understood God to be the guiding force behind the planets, as well as the Creator of the entire universe. In the Hebrew commentaries known as the Talmud, archangels are usually associated with astronomical phenomena. That may have been the case in the destruction of the Assyrian army.

> Then the angel of the LORD went out and put to death a hundred and eighty-five thousand men in the Assyrian camp. When the people got up the next morning — there were all the dead bodies! (Isa. 37:36).

Another well-known Hebrew piece of literature, the book of Enoch, assigns seven archangels the governorships of the sun, the moon and the luminaries. In some passages, certain archangels are assigned to specific planets. The archangels in Hebrew literature are the corresponding figures to the planet deities of ancient non-Hebrew literature.

In Hebrew theology, the controller of the archangels is God; whereas in pagan religions, such as those of the Greeks or Chaldeans, the planets themselves are deities. However, because of the influence of the heathen nations, which God warned the Hebrews against, the Hebrews were often led astray and worshiped the heathen gods such as Baal and Ashtoreth. They suffered immensely for their disobedience.

What Changed the Calendar.

By the sixth century B.C., something unusual had happened in the heavens, because the Greek mathematician Thales (640-546 B.C.) recorded a new latitude, a new number of days for the year, a new path of the sun, and a new lunar period for the country of Greece. These are all indications that the heavens had been in a state of cosmic disturbance.

By the time the philosopher Socrates (470-399 B.C.) came on the scene, doubt regarding the truth of the planets being gods began to be an issue of debate. It doesn't take long for questions to arise by any generation concerning previous events — especially those that the rational and logical mind has a hard time assimilating. Such was the case with the Pharisees concerning the man who was born blind and was healed by Jesus (Jn. 9). The Pharisees' skeptical minds could not conceive of miracles, let alone accept Jesus as the Messiah.

With the cessation of frequent celestial-related catastrophes after 700 B.C., Greek civilization began to flower. Philosophy, debate and the analytical approach to life became the order of the day. Worship of the planets declined, not because Greek thinkers had become more intelligent, but because civilization was disrupted no more by catastrophe from the heavens. The study of astronomy and astrology was no longer critical to national survival, so there was a drastic drop in the interest shown in the subjects.

It is rather interesting to see that of late there has been a revival in the study of astronomy as well as in astrology as a science, even by government-supported industries such as the National Aeronautics and Space Administration (NASA). NASA is receiving billions of tax dollars to once again research and chart the movements of objects in the heavens for the safety of planet Earth. The hope is to protect mankind against any threat of a potentially deadly cosmic visitor, such as an asteroid. That is what is believed to have led to the extinction of the dinosaurs. According to the words of Christ, such a doomsday is soon to occur once again on planet Earth.

Paul and Mars Hill.

By Paul's time, A.D. 50, Mars Hill (see fig. #101) in Athens had lost its original importance and significance. It was on this very hill, which was earlier dedicated to the god of Mars, that Paul debated with the Greeks regarding the resurrection of Christ.

The city of Rome was also dedicated to the celestial war-god, Mars, with annual festivals in his honor. It was founded in 750 B.C., a few decades before peace came to the heavens. On the original Roman calendar, the first month of the year was March, named in honor of Mars.

By 364 B.C., astronomical events had been forgotten, and the Roman calendar was reorganized so that no longer was March 21 the first day of the new year. January 1, which celebrated the winter solstice when the sun began to return northward, became the first day of the year.

Plutarch, the Greek author (A.D. 46-120),

Figure #101. MARS HILL

wrote in his book, *Life of Numa*, that the ancient Roman calendar had 360 days in the year during the eighth century B.C., and each month had 30 days. It was after the 701 B.C. holocaust that a year became 365¼ days long.

Numa, who was the king of Rome after the heavenly holocaust, had to reorganize the calendar; he added five days per year. Numa's contemporary, King Hezekiah of Jerusalem, made a different kind of adjustment. He added one month every six years, an adjustment which rabbis later recorded. Numa named the first four months of the year at the time after four of the visible planets: March in honor of Mars, April or Aprilla in honor of Venus, May or Maius in honor of Mercury, and June or Juno in honor of Jupiter. India, Persia, Chaldea, Assyria, Egypt, Greece, and Rome are just a few of the ancient civilizations which once had a 360-day calendar.

Stonehenge.

In Northern Europe, the planet gods were worshiped from 2000 B.C. to 500 B.C. These deities were of primary importance in the folklore of that region. Hundreds of astronomical temples were erected in Great Britain alone during this era. The most well-known is Stonehenge, which was erected between 1900 B.C. and 1600 B.C.

This temple was built to help the ancient priesthood predict eclipses and planetary movements, as well as other celestial-related phenomena. Like the Olympic deities in Greece and the planetary worship in Rome, later generations in England forgot the long past catastrophic scene, but Stonehenge remains as a reminder that it played a huge role in the lives of the ancients.

Chapter Fifty-Two

The Gods on Our Calendars

Figure #102. CALENDAR GODS

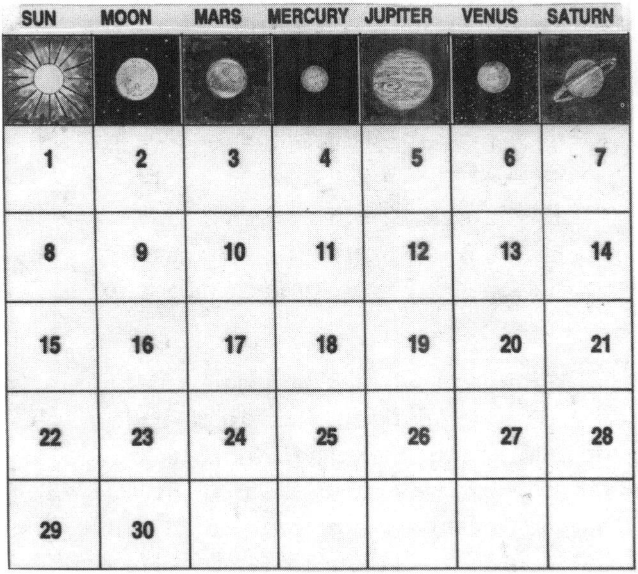

SUN	MOON	MARS	MERCURY	JUPITER	VENUS	SATURN
1	2	3	4	5	6	7
8	9	10	11	12	13	14
15	16	17	18	19	20	21
22	23	24	25	26	27	28
29	30					

Worshiping the Gods of the Week.

As a result of celestial worship by the ancient
Europeans, the days of their week were named

in honor of the five visible planets and included the sun and moon of the Earth. To this day, the names remain the same in the Western world. They are as follows (notice the closeness in the Spanish language):

1. Sun-daeg or Sunday
2. Moon-daeg or Monday, (moon is luna, Lunes in Spanish)
3. Tiwes-daeg or Tuesday, Mars' day, (Martes in Spanish)
4. Odens-daeg or Wednesday, Mercury's day, (Miercoles in Spanish)
5. Thors-daeg or Thursday, Jupiter's day, (Jueves in Spanish)
6. Preyia-daeg or Friday, Venus' day, (Viernes in Spanish)
7. Saturn's-day or Saturday, (Sabado in Spanish)

In England, March (named in honor of Mars) was considered the first month of the legal year up until as recently as 1752. March was the lengthened month instead of February. In Scotland, January replaced March as the first month in 1599. In France, March was recognized as the first month until 1564, when Charles IX by edict decreed January the first month instead of March.

The same is true in Asia regarding the days of the week often being named after the planets.

	Korean		Chinese	
Monday	월 Wol	(일 = day)	月 (Moon)	= Moon
Tuesday	화 Wha	"	火 (Fire)	= Mars
Wednesday	수 Soo	"	水 (Water)	= Mercury
Thursday	목 Mok	"	木 (Tree)	= Jupiter
Friday	금 Kum-(Gm)	"	金 (Gold)	= Venus
Saturday	토 Tto	"	土 (Land)	= Saturn
Sunday	일 Il	"	日 (Sun)	= Sun
	성 (Sung)		星 (Sung)	= Star

Figure #103. HALLOWED NIGHT

Chapter Fifty-Three

Halloween and Friday the 13th

Hallowed Evening.

In Great Britain, Ireland and the United States, ancient Halloween folk customs persist in the month of October and bring billions of dollars in business. This includes a long and deep tradition of bad luck, black cats, witches on broomsticks in the sky, astrologies, cosmic rites and so forth.

These Halloween rituals can be traced to worship of Baal and Ashtoreth, the deities for Mars and Venus. It was believed that many of the ancient catastrophes occurred or threatened on or about October 25. Halloween means hallowed evening or holy evening. Friday the 13th is another fragment of the ancients' fear related to catastrophes that came from the cosmos.

14th Day of Nisan.

Scripture reveals that the catastrophes of

338 JOSHUA'S LONG DAY AND JONAH'S LONG NIGHT

Sodom and Gomorrah, the final plague of the Exodus, and the catastrophe which occurred during Isaiah's life and others, fell on the evening preceding the 14th of the month of Nisan. The 14th of Nisan always fell on Saturday on the Hebrew calendar. So Friday the 13th became a night of dread and a day of ill luck.

Thank the Lord for Psalm 91 and the blood of Christ on the doorposts of believers' hearts and minds. They guard against any death angel, plague, or calamity, no matter on which day Satan plans them to fall.

Conclusion.

Regular catastrophic events deeply affected the lives of the ancients. Since we do not experience this today, it is easy to attribute the ancient traditions to nothing more than pagan ignorance. Apparently, great celestial disturbances did occur in ancient times. This would be the case if some of the celestial bodies in the ancient solar system had intersecting orbits and hence, there was great potential for catastrophic encounters. Perhaps hairy comets were involved in this interplay with Earth.

Chapter Fifty-Four

Cosmic Warfare and Hairy Comets

When the Sky Fell.

Could it be that for a time after the Great Flood, our planet or some other astral body was in a different orbit than it is presently? If, for example, another planet in our solar system, such as Mars were in an elliptical orbit, then the effects upon planet Earth could be catastrophic. **(See fig. #104.)** Once calculations were made, catastrophic occurrences could have been predicted.

Mars was considered by many ancient people

Figure #104. VISITOR FOR A SEASON

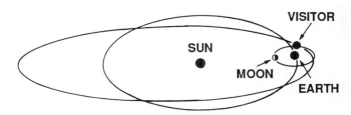

as the deity of war. Archaeology has revealed the god Baal (mentioned in the Bible) was associated with this war god, Mars. That may explain why many of the ancients' calendars named the first month of the year March; it was done in honor of Mars. Was this why Rome was founded and dedicated to the celestial god Mars — with annual festivals given in his honor?

If Mars was in an ancient orbit — one different than its present orbit, it may have caused the fragmentation of a former planet, the remnants of which are known today as the "asteroids." Two of these asteroids were captured by Mars' gravitational field and still orbit the red planet. They are its tiny moons known as Demos and Phobos. **(See fig. #105.)** Many of these asteroids have pounded the surface of Mars, Mercury, the Earth and its moon, and the other planets, as mentioned in chapter 29.

Under such circumstances, it is easy to understand why the ancients would have prayed to and worshiped Mars and Thor (Jupiter, called the father of Mars). Mars was Baal, the god of fire and destruction, who needed placating, and this was accomplished by sacrificing children. Venus, on the other hand, was Ashtoreth, the goddess of restoration and fertility, whom the pagans worshiped by having sex orgies.

Figure #105. DEMOS AND PHOBOS

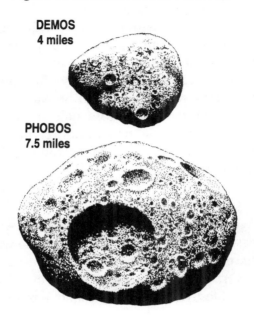

DEMOS
4 miles

PHOBOS
7.5 miles

Associated with the worship of Ashtoreth and Baal were astrological omens, incantations, licentious rituals, sacrificial murders, orgiastic music, sorceries and witchcraft. If catastrophe came, it was rationalized that an insufficient number of sacrifices had been made.

The night before the ancient city of Carthage fell, it was reported by the Roman troops that one could smell the burning of flesh, presumably

Carthaginian children being sacrificed. This obsession to appease the angry gods of the cosmos is apparently the reason for the worldwide construction of so many ancient sun or planet temples, obelisks, gnomons and sun caves.

Now we can see why so many of the ancient civilizations were involved in human sacrifice — and why they came to a sudden end. God brought sudden disasters on whole civilizations, wiping them out because of their hideous religious practices.

The Golden Calf.

What caused God to be so angry that He wanted to destroy the children of Israel when Moses was on the mountain receiving the Ten Commandments (Ex. 32)? The Israelites were involved in a sexually immoral festival and idol worship of a golden calf made by Aaron, the priest.

The ancient Egyptians and the Canaanites worshiped the god, Baal (Mars), symbolized as a bull. No doubt the Israelites, who had just come out of Egypt, found it quite natural to make an image that symbolized power and fertility. They had just been delivered from their enemies by great miraculous events, some of which were associated with the heavens. But their Deliverer was God, and He had commanded them not to make any images symbolizing "anything in heaven above or on the earth beneath" (Ex. 20:4).

The Hair-Tailed Comet. (See fig. #106.)

Some scholars have suggested an alternative to the basis for the ancients becoming terrified by heavenly bodies. They believe it was Venus rather than Mars that caused astral catastrophes.

As previously mentioned, *Worlds in Collisions*, written by Immanuel Velikovsky in the 1940s, documents catastrophic events recorded by ancients from

Figure #106. HAIRY COMET

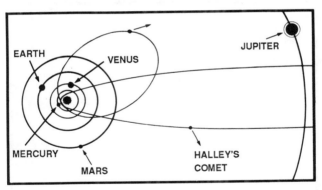

around the world. Velikovsky believed these catastrophic events corresponded to the judgments recorded in Scripture. A brief summary of these events was noted in the *Reader's Digest.* [25]

Velikovsky's investigation into the historical

records of the ancients led him to conclude that around 4,000 years ago, people around the world witnessed the appearance of a brand new heavenly body in the form of a comet. This comet came near to the Earth every 52 years. On several of these close encounters, the Earth passed through the tail of the comet, which brought about terrible devastation to the Earth. **(See fig. #107.)** As mentioned in Chapter 29,

Figure #107. CATACLYSMIC TAILS

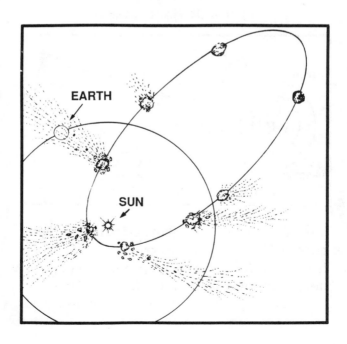

even today the Earth passes through remnants of comet trails known as meteor streams.

The ancients were quite terrified of this ancient body and began to worship it and sacrifice to it as a god as it became dominant in the heavens. Sometime around the seventh century B.C., this comet was deflected out of its comet orbit into a planetary orbit, and Velikovsky believes it became what we now call the planet Venus.

Venus and the Ancients.

The ancients recorded the following about the comet:

The Chaldeans: "Queen of Heaven;" "Bright torch of Heaven"

The Sumarians: "Rains flaming fire over the land"

The Assyrians: "Fearful dragon ... clothed in fire"

The Egyptians: "The star with hair"

The Persians: "The goddess of destruction;" "A circling star which scatters its flame in fire." "Tried to destroy the human race."

The Greeks: "Blazing star;" nearly destroyed the world with fire, and then was transformed into the planet Venus.

From India: Looked like "fire and smoke;" it hurled fire upon heaven and earth"

The Chinese: Venus rivaled the sun for brightness.

The Indians of Mexico: Venus was called the star that smoked; when it appeared a great number of people died of famine and pestilence. The Aztec calendar was used to plot the 52-year cycle.

The Indians of Peru: The "wavy-haired" star.

The Hebrews: From the Talmud: "Fire is hanging down from the planet Venus."

From the Midrash: "The brilliant light of Venus blazes from one end of the cosmos to the other."

From the Bible: Some scholars maintain that "Mazzaroth" in Job 38:32 (NKJV) may literally mean "bearded star."

The reason the ancients called comets "hair stars" is that from their perspective on the Earth, the tail looked like a long flowing head of hair. The English word "comet" comes from the Greek word "komet," which means the long-haired one or the star with hair. The Greek Septuagint of the Old Testament indicates that Venus was a "hair star" in the days of Job.

Predictions About Venus Come to Light.

Whether or not Velikovsky's conclusions are

correct is still a matter of speculation. However, in the late 1940s, long before probes were sent into space, he made several predictions about what would be discovered about Venus. One was mentioned in Chapter 22: The planet would have a shortage of craters. He based his beliefs upon what the ancients said about Venus — that it was a comet and then became a planet. He believed the following about Venus:

1. It would have the remains of a tail.
2. It would have a high surface temperature.
3. It would have a dense, heavy atmosphere.
4. It would have hydrocarbons in its atmosphere.

These ideas were nonsense to evolutionists because they believed Venus was formed when all the other planets of our solar system were formed. However, every one of Velikovsky's conclusions proved to be true.

1. Mariner 2 (1962) found a high temperature: 480 Celsius.
2. Venera 3 (1966) found a very dense and heavy atmosphere.
3. Mariner 10 (1974) found remains of a comet tail.
4. Mariner 10 (1974) found that there were hydrocarbons in the atmosphere.

5. Magellan Space Probe found a shortage of craters.

Passing Through the Tail.

Question: How did Venus bring destruction to planet Earth? We know Venus' tail was made up of debris of various sizes. This meteorite material was composed of much iron and dust, along with hydrocarbons. Hydrocarbons are the bases of petroleum products such as tar and oil. A close encounter would have polluted the Earth's atmosphere with iron dust particles, turning the atmosphere a reddish color. Meteorite showers would have struck the Earth, and friction could have melted the iron material into a molten state — like hot lava. Hydrocarbons are flammable.

So when the Bible speaks about fire and brimstone destruction, it is talking about fire from hydrocarbons, the brimstone being hot rock. Now we have a basis for the destruction which fell upon Sodom and Gomorrah and other similar catastrophes spoken of in the Scriptures.

In Job 38:32 (NKJV) we read, "Can you bring out Mazzaroth in its season (orbit)? Or can you guide the Great Bear?" A word study on Mazzaroth reveals that it could be Venus. "Season" means orbit, and Venus is still known as the evening star today.[26]

Plagues Falling Upon the Earth.

If at one time the planet Venus was in an orbit which passed the Earth every 50 years or so, imagine the effects it would have had on the Earth's tides? The magma inside our globe would have been affected, causing volcanoes to erupt, spewing ash into the atmosphere, blocking the sun's rays, resulting in darkness. There would have been earthquakes, axis shifts, mountain ranges thrusting up, crustal movements, exchanges in electrical discharges, and the rising and sinking of land masses, causing water displacement and erosion. All this would have terrified the ancients living after the Flood, motivating them to try to appease these angry gods. Thus they delved into planetary worship.

Chapter Fifty-Five

What if We Had Been Alive in Those Days?

Summary.

If the theory of astral catastrophism is true, we can understand why there was so much cosmic warfare involved in ancient mythology, why temples dedicated to astronomical related phenomena were constructed, and why planet gods were worshiped by various civilizations all over the world from about 2000 B.C. to 500 B.C. It also gives us insight as to why the days of the week have been named after the sun, moon and planets, and what led to the first four months of the ancient calendar being named in honor of these deitized heavenly bodies.

Had we been alive from the time of Noah's Flood (approximately 2500 B.C.), through the dispersion of people to the nations during the construction of the Tower of Babel (approximately 1900 B.C.), observing the great civilizations of the ancient world — the Chinese, Egyptians, Babylonians, Assyrians, Persians, Aztecs, Mayas and Incas — and their construction of great temples, until around 700 B.C., we would have been profoundly aware of the catastrophic dangers associated with the heavens.

Had we lived on through the times of the Greek empire, we would have insight as to why so much of ancient mythology was about the planetary gods that were constantly raining destruction upon mortal man. Had we lived on until the day of the Apostle Paul, we would even understand why the place where he spoke to the Athenians was called Mars Hill; it was dedicated to the planetary war god, Mars.

So much of ancient history has been labeled mythology because the ancients associated their stories with the gods of the heavens. However, once we realize that the heavens were, in fact, out of sync, causing periodical havoc and destruction on planet Earth, we have a new understanding — not only of what has been called mythology, but of biblical passages describing judgments coming from the heavens. In addition, we gain a new perspective to the puzzling astronomical phenomena mentioned in the previous sections and the following one titled, "The Coming Holocaust."

SECTION VIII
THE COMING HOLOCAUST

Chapter 56: The Doomsday Asteroid
Chapter 57: A Foretaste of the Final
             Judgment
Chapter 58: Consider the Ominous Words
             of Jesus
Chapter 59: Revelation and the Coming
             Judgment
Conclusion: You be the Judge

Figure #108. DOOMSDAY ASTEROID

Chapter Fifty-Six

The Doomsday Asteroid

Hard Rock From Outer Space.

In 1996, the television science program *Nova* reported the speculation about coming catastrophe to planet Earth. The hour-long program was titled, *The Doomsday Asteroid*, and the 1997 National Geographic television special, *Asteroids Deadly Impact* adds even more spectacular evidence.

Had the explosion over Siberia in 1908 hit a populated area like New York City, it would have devastated the entire area, killing millions of people. More than a hundred craters made by the impact of meteors have now been identified on the surface of the Earth. One of them is Meteor Crater, which is located in Arizona. **(See fig. #109.)**

Astronomers and archaeologists are now confirming that the heavens are a source of potential disaster. It seems that the asteroid belt

Figure #109. METEOR CRATER, ARIZONA

sends asteroid missiles to various parts of our solar system. It is believed that one of the mechanisms for launching these missiles is Jupiter's gravitational field, which continually perturbs these asteroids.

The *Nova* program stated that 90% of the Earth-crossing asteroids have yet to be discovered. During the '50s and '60s, postulated threats from space took the form of extraterrestrials such as the little green men known as "the Martians." In the '70s and '80s, *Star Trek*, *Space Invaders* and *The Adventures of Star Wars* took center stage. Today the picture has changed dramatically. Science fiction is no longer captivating the film industry. The threat today is as real as flesh and blood — only it is recognized as "hard rock from outer space."

What all this means is that a huge piece of rock or rocks could bring devastation to the Earth. It is estimated that there are several hundred thousand potentially dangerous asteroids that are bigger than the one that devastated Siberia. There are at least 2,000 that are larger than half a mile in diameter, and there are 100 million that are larger than 10 meters. At the current rate of locating and cataloging the asteroids that are a half-mile in diameter or larger, it will take the next 200-300 years to complete the task. If during that time, one of those asteroids not yet recorded should head for Earth, its arrival would be a surprise.

God's 1993 July Fireworks Show.

In 1993, two men, Shoemaker and Levy, discovered a string of 21 comets on a collision course with Jupiter. The comets smashed into Jupiter on July 16, 1994 and were dubbed the cosmic collision of the century.

Their speed was about 130,000 miles an hour, and the minimum size of the largest fragments was about a third of a mile. They hit with a force half a million times greater than the Siberian explosion. Each impact left a scar the size of planet Earth!

According to David Levy, "If the comet and its 21 pieces were to hit the Earth, I think the human race would survive it. But the devastation and the suffering would be beyond belief. To say it would be the largest natural disaster ever seen by humanity is to understate it. The death of people would be probably counted in the billions. We'd probably lose a substantial number of people through starvation, cold and misery. But not everyone would die. The planet would survive and things would come back. But it might be that the survivors might actually envy the dead for at least a while."

There is no means of predicting such an event happening to our planet. Astronomers now recognize that the universe is not the tranquil home they once thought. Earth is vulnerable, and some day, catastrophe will hit once again. **(See fig. #110.)**

Figure #110. COSMIC COLLISION

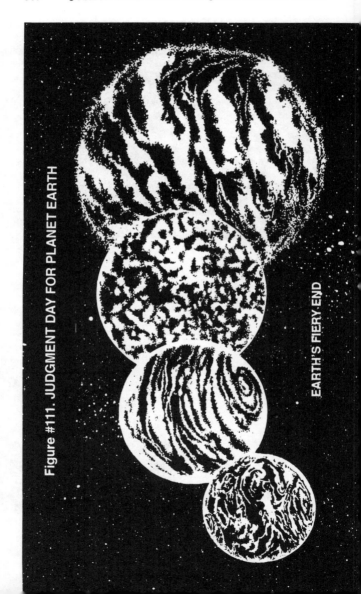

Figure #111. JUDGMENT DAY FOR PLANET EARTH

EARTH'S FIERY END

Chapter Fifty-Seven

A Foretaste of the Final Judgment

Lest We Forget.

The Genesis Flood was a catastrophic event and a prototype of the final judgment awaiting this present world. It was a foretaste of events yet to come.

> For the coming of the Son of Man will be just like the days of Noah. For as in those days which were before the flood they were eating and drinking, they were marrying and giving in marriage, until the day that NOAH ENTERED THE ARK, and they did not understand until the flood came and took them all away, so shall the coming of the Son of Man be (Matt. 24:37-39 NASV).

The Great Flood happened because people

disobeyed God. Only Noah and his family obeyed Him, and they were saved. Just as it was in the days of Noah, so it will be in the days preceding the coming catastrophe and the return of Christ.

II Peter 3 reveals that there will be skeptics who claim there will be no end to the world, that everything will continue as it is now. Peter told his audience to remember the account of Noah's ark and the Flood. He then warned of a final destruction of this world and the heavens by fire. Peter advised the people to repent and to accept salvation offered by the Messiah, Jesus.

> But the day of the Lord will come like a thief. The heavens will disappear with a roar; the elements will be destroyed by fire, and the earth and everything in it will be laid bare. ... That day will bring about the destruction of the heavens by fire, and the elements will melt in the heat (II Pet. 3:10,12). **(See fig. #112.)**

Even the people of Nineveh, as Jesus pointed out, will one day bear witness against those nations who refuse the message of the "one greater than Jonah" (Matt. 12:41).

Figure #112. THE FIERY END

Chapter Fifty-Eight

Consider the Ominous Words of Jesus

The Coming Catastrophe.

The Bible graphically reveals that planet Earth has experienced a series of awesome and devastating catastrophes, and that it is fast approaching another series of worldwide catastrophic events. The disaster that occurred during Joshua's day, and even the one which was withheld during Jonah's day, are but a forewarning of catastrophic events yet to come to Earth.

The same literary style describing Old Testament catastrophes reappears in the New Testament. The cataclysmic judgments spoken of in the Old Testament help us understand Christ's apocalyptic teaching in the Gospels. The 10 plagues of Exodus are a sort of catastrophic parallel for the coming world holocausts described in Revelation. Ezekiel's prophetic chapters, 38 and 39, give a vivid description of fire and brimstone catastrophisms in the "end times," falling not on the Amorites and Assyrian armies, but on the armies invading Israel from the north. When God's fireworks begin, man's fireworks are puny in comparison. Consider the words of Jesus in the following passages:

Falling Stars: Matthew 24:29. (See fig. #113.)

> Immediately after the distress of those days "the sun will be darkened, and the moon will not give its light; **the stars will fall from the sky, and the heavenly bodies will be shaken**."

This verse sounds amazingly similar to what evolutionists now believe led to the extinction of the Age of the Dinosaurs. A giant meteorite supposedly plunged into the Earth and emitted pulverized ash into the stratosphere, resulting in the blockage of sunlight. Such an event is similar to what the Bible predicts will occur in the near future.

Terrifying Events in the Heavens: Luke 21:8-11,25 (LB).

> He replied, "Don't let anyone mislead you. For many will come announcing

Figure #113. TARGET EARTH

themselves as the Messiah, and saying, 'The time has come.' But don't believe them! And when you hear of wars and insurrections beginning, don't panic. True, wars must come, but the end won't follow immediately — for nation shall rise against nation and kingdom against kingdom, and there will be great earthquakes, and famines in many lands, and epidemics, and **terrifying things happening in the heavens. ... Then there will be strange events in the skies — warnings, evil omens and portents in the sun, moon and stars."**

What could be more "terrifying" than knowing of a cosmic visitor on target to intersect with our planet and having the potential to cause havoc to part or all of planet Earth? **(See fig. #114.)** The above passage of Scripture seems to imply that such an event will be associated with the events leading up to the end of history on this planet.

Roaring Seas and Strange Tides: Luke 21:25,26 (LB).

Down here on earth the nations will be in turmoil, perplexed by the **roaring**

Figure #114. DESTINATION PLANET EARTH

seas and strange tides. The courage
of many people will falter because of
the fearful fate they see coming upon
the earth, for **the stability of the very
heavens will be broken up**.

Notice how people will be perplexed by the
"roaring seas and strange tides." This definitely
suggests an unusually strong gravitational
attraction caused by a large cosmic visitor. But

lest we be fearful, the following verses reveal the coming of the Messiah in power and glory:

> Then the peoples of the earth shall see me, the Messiah, coming in a cloud with power and great glory. So when all these things begin to happen, stand straight and look up! For your salvation is near (Lk. 21:27,28 LB).

Outline of Prophetic Forecast.

Jesus' prophetic forecast from the books of Matthew and Luke is a description of what seems to be coming from the heavens, causing catastrophic reactions such as:

1. Powerful gravitational forces
2. Meteorite explosions — high winds
3. A flexing and separating of the Earth's crust — earthquake activity
4. Volcanic eruptions everywhere
5. Mountain ranges being leveled
6. Oceanic tides rising
7. The end of the present Earth

Once again we see another chapter of the *Original Star Wars* described in graphic detail in John's apocalyptic Revelation. It appears that the catastrophic judgments of Joshua's Long Day and Jonah's Long Night will again come to planet Earth.

Chapter Fifty-Nine

Revelation and the Coming Judgment

The Apostle John had a taste of virtual reality long before it was invented by man. While John was on the island of Patmos, the Holy Spirit revealed to him the earthshaking events which would take place at the end of time — just prior to the trumpet blast when the Creator of the Universe will suddenly arrive on the scene. Several upheavals will take place to set the stage for the Messiah's return.

It is amazing how some of the passages in Revelation resemble those in Joshua 10. The heavens will be once again be associated with the cataclysmic events on the Earth. And in this case, it will be the end of time. Cosmic visitors in the form of meteorites, comets, asteroids and plane-toids will bring judgment to the people of the Earth. If it happened in the past, it can happen again. When and how we cannot be sure, but if the Bible declares it, we can be certain it will come to pass.

A World Gone Mad: Revelation 6:12-17 (LB).

I watched as he broke the sixth seal, and there was a vast earthquake; and the sun became dark like black cloth, and the moon was blood-red. **Then the stars of heaven appeared to be falling to earth (see fig. #115) — like green fruit from fig trees buffeted by mighty winds. And the starry heavens disappeared as though rolled up like a scroll and taken away; and**

Figure #115. D-DAY PLANET EARTH

every mountain and island shook and shifted. The kings of the earth, and world leaders and rich men, and high-ranking military officers, and all men great and small, slave and free, hid themselves in the caves and rocks of the mountains, and cried to the mountains to crush them. "Fall on us." they pleaded, "and hide us from the face of the one sitting on the throne, and from the anger of the Lamb, because the great day of their anger has come, and who can survive it?"

One-Third of Earth Set on Fire: Revelation 8:5-9 (LB).

Then the angel filled the censer with fire from the altar and threw it down upon the earth; and thunder crashed and rumbled, lightning flashed, and there was a terrible earthquake. Then the seven angels with the seven trumpets prepared to blow their mighty blasts. The first angel blew his trumpet, and **hail and fire mixed with blood were thrown down upon the earth. One-third of the earth was set on fire so that one-third of the trees**

were burned, and all the green
grass. (See fig. #116.) Then the second

Figure #116. HELLSTORM

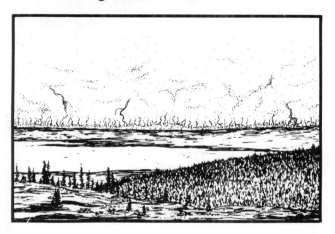

angel blew his trumpet, and **what appeared to be a huge burning mountain was thrown into the sea** (see fig.
#117), **destroying a third of all the
ships; and a third of the sea turned
red as blood; and a third of the fish
were killed**.

The "Bitter" Soviet Nuclear Disaster: Revelation 8:10,11 (LB).

The third angel blew, and **a great
flaming star fell from the heaven**

Figure #117. COSMIC HOLOCAUST

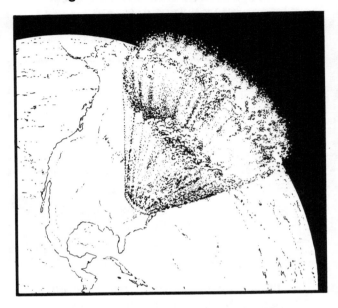

upon a third of the rivers and springs. The star was called "Bitterness" because it poisoned a third of all the water on the earth and many people died.

It is significant that the word for "bitterness" here means "wormwood." That is the exact meaning of Chernobyl, which is the name of the place in the former Soviet Union where the nuclear disaster occurred a number of years ago.

The ground and the atmosphere became contaminated as a result of the radioactive fallout. The Bible says that a star called "bitterness" or "wormwood" will fall, and a third of the Earth's water will be contaminated.

> The fourth angel blew his trumpet and immediately a third of the sun was blighted and darkened, and a third of the moon and the stars, so that the daylight was dimmed by a third, and the night-time darkness deepened (Rev. 8:12 LB).

Could it be that this darkness will be caused by volcanic ash being spewed into the stratosphere?

The Heavens are Darkened: Revelation 9:1,2 (LB).

> Then the fifth angel blew his trumpet and I saw one who was fallen to earth from heaven, and to him was given the key to the bottomless pit. When he opened it, smoke poured out as though from some huge furnace, and the sun and air were darkened by the smoke.

A Meteorite Shower: Revelation 16:8-11 (LB).

> Then the fourth angel poured out his

flask upon the sun **(see fig. #118),**

Figure #118. TONGUES OF FIRE

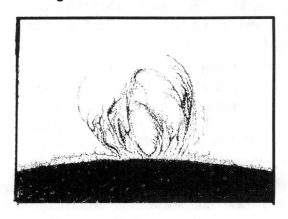

causing it to scorch all men with its fire. Everyone was burned by this blast of heat, and they cursed the name of God who sent the plagues — they did not change their mind and attitude to give Him glory. Then the fifth angel poured out his flask upon the throne of the Creature from the sea, and his kingdom was plunged into darkness. And his subjects gnawed their tongues in anguish, and cursed the God of heaven for their pains and sores, but they refused to repent of all their evil deeds.

9.8 on the Richter Scale: Revelation 16:17-21 (LB).

> Then the seventh angel poured out his flask into the air; and a mighty shout came from the throne of the temple in heaven, saying, "It is finished!" Then the thunder crashed and rolled, and lightning flashed; and there was a great earthquake of a magnitude unprecedented in human history. The great city of "Babylon" split into three sections, and cities around the world fell in heaps of rubble (see **fig. #119**); and so all of "Babylon's" sins were

Figure #119. 9.8 MAGNITUDE

remembered in God's thoughts, and she was punished to the last drop of anger in the cup of the wine of the fierceness of his wrath. And islands vanished, and mountains flattened out, and there was an incredible hailstorm from heaven; hailstones weighing a hundred pounds fell from the sky onto the people below, and they cursed God because of the terrible hail **(see fig. #120)**.

Once again, there is mention of "hailstones" falling from heaven. We think of hailstones as being composed of ice because we've never seen

Figure #120. 100-POUND HAILSTONES

hot rocks falling from the sky. However, when we read about each stone weighing in at 100 pounds, then we need to think in terms of hot rock rather than "hot ice."

The heaviest hailstones of ice ever recorded fell in Bangladesh in 1986. They weighed only $2\frac{1}{4}$ pounds, but they killed 92 people. Although large chunks of ice are capable of killing people, their destructive power is a far cry from what an avalanche of 100-pound meteorite rocks will do.

Imagine the damage that will occur to both man and machine when these huge stones begin dropping out of the heavens as Revelation predicts. A $2\frac{1}{4}$-pound object would be only about the size of a cantaloupe. A 100-pound hailstone would be 25 times larger — about the size of a watermelon two feet by one foot. (See fig. #121.)

This description in Revelation of a meteorite shower coming out of the heavens is on the order of the destructive meteorite catastrophes which annihilated Sodom and Gomorrah, the Ammorites of Joshua's day, and the Assyrian army during Hezekiah's day (Isa. 37).

Notice that when the heavens began raining down such incredible judgment, instead of falling on their faces and crying out for mercy, the people cursed God. Here is another example

Figure #121. CANTELOUPES VERSUS WATERMELONS

of a just judgment on a wicked and depraved people who have totally rejected God.

End-Time Catastrophes Associated With the Heavens.

According to Revelation, as the end of time approaches, the Earth will experience major catastrophes associated with the heavens. Although we may be concerned about the coming events which we read in Revelation, we do not have to be afraid. Just as God protected the children of Israel in the land of Goshen in Egypt during the plagues which fell on the Egyptians, so it will be at the end time. God will have His "Goshens" in which He will protect His children when these events begin to take place. **(See fig. #122.)**

Figure #122. THE SHEPHERD AND HIS SHEEP

Conclusion

You be the Judge

You be the Judge.

Are the accounts of Joshua's Long Day and Jonah's Long Night mere myths?

A young believer was talking to a skeptic about the reliability and inspiration of the Bible. The skeptic sarcastically remarked, "You don't really believe that story about a fish swallowing Jonah, do you?" To which the young Christian replied, "Yes, there are some difficult things which I don't fully understand yet, but I plan to ask Jonah when I see him in heaven." "And what if Jonah isn't in heaven?" asked the infidel. "Then you ask him," replied the believer.

Is your account balanced in heaven? Don't be like the infidel.

> Blessed is the man who does not walk
> in the counsel of the wicked or stand
> in the way of sinners or sit in the seat
> of mockers. But his delight is in the

law of the LORD, and on his law he meditates day and night (Psa 1:1,2).

He will judge the world in righteousness; he will govern the peoples with justice (Psa. 9:8).

For he has set a day when he will judge the world with justice by the man he has appointed. He has given proof of this to all men by raising him (Christ) from the dead (Acts 17:31).

And I saw the dead, great and small, standing before the throne, and books were opened. Another book was opened, which is the book of life. The dead were judged according to what they had done as recorded in the books. The sea gave up the dead that were in it, and death and Hades gave up the dead that were in them, and each person was judged according to what he had done. Then death and Hades were thrown into the lake of fire. The lake of fire is the second death. If anyone's name was not found written in the book of life, he was thrown into the lake of fire (Rev. 20:12-15).

> For God so loved the world that he gave his one and only Son, that whoever believes in him shall not perish but have eternal life. For God did not send his Son into the world to condemn the world, but to save the world through him (Jn. 3:16,17).

God is not willing that anyone should perish, but desires everyone to come to repentance (II Pet. 3:9).

Endnotes

1. *Rivers in the Desert*, (New York: Farrar, Strauss and Cudahy, 1959), p. 31.

2. The age of the Earth and the fallacies associated with radiometric dating techniques are covered in Volumes VIII and IX of the Creation Science Series.

3. *Science Digest*, (August 1986) p. 71.

4. *Dallas Times Herald*, (Thursday, May 7, 1981), a-31.

5. Scientifically, there is always measurable electromagnetic radiation wherever you have any matter at all at a temperature above absolute zero. But such radiation is usually not visible light unless the matter is at a fairly high temperature. Scripture does indicate that the first three days were divided into light and darkness.

6. *National Geographic*, (June 1996).

7. Immanuel Velikovsky, *Worlds in Collision*, (New York: Doubleday & Company Inc.,

1950). Immanuel Velikovsky, *Earth in Upheaval*, (New York: Doubleday & Company Inc., 1968).

8.   Such subject matter will be discussed in Volume XI of the Creation Science Series on the mysteries of the ancients.

9.   *Science News*, (June 28, 1980).

10.   Volume VI of the Creation Science Series entitled, *The Original Star Wars and the Age of Ice*, lays a foundation for understanding the significance of this volume. There are many additional passages within the Bible where God brings judgment upon wicked nations by using natural disasters which originate in the heavens.

11.   Louis Ginzberg, *The Legends of the Jews*, Vol. IV, (Philadelphia: The Jewish Publication Society of America, 1913), p. 12.

12.   Once again it is advisable to read Volume VI in conjunction with this volume. Numerous catastrophes in Scripture that can be attributed to forces in the heavens are covered in Volume VI of the Creation Science Series entitled, *The Original Star Wars and the Age of Ice*.

13. Material for this chapter was obtained from the following sources:

    a.   Barry Setterfield, *Astronomical Evidence for the Flood*.

    b.   Ex Nihilo

        (1) Carl Wieland, *An Asteroid Tilts the Earth*, (January 1983).

        (2) Barry Setterfield, *An Asteroid Tilts the Earth*, (April 1983).

14. M.M. Noah and A.S. Gould, *The Book of Jashar*, (New York: 1840).

15. M.M. Noah and A.S. Gould, *The Book of Jashar*, (New York: 1840), p. 260.

16. World in Collision (New York: Doubleday, 1950), p. 401. *Bible-Science Newsletter*, (July 1989, Vol. 27, No. 7) also documents many of these parallel events of Joshua's Long Day.

17. The construction of these ancient mysteries in the light of the Bible is covered in Volume XI of the Creation Science Series, *The Genesis Man and His Amazing Accomplishments*.

18. Material for this chapter was obtained from the following sources:

    a.   Barry Setterfield, *Astronomical*

Evidence for the Flood.

b.   Ex Nihilo

(1)   Carl Wieland, *An Asteroid Tilts the Earth*, (January 1983).

(2)   Barry Setterfield, *An Asteroid Tilts the Earth*, (April 1983).

19.   *Encyclopedia Britannica*, Vol. 17, (Chicago: William Benton, Publisher, 1958), p. 687. The story is most fully told in the *Metamorphoses of Ovid*, (i, 750, ii, 366, and Nonnus, Dionysiaca, xxxviii).

20.   Harry Rimmer, *The Harmony of Science and Scripture*, (Grand Rapids: Eerdmans Publishing Co., 1936), Chapter 5.

21.   Bernard Ramm, *The Christian View of Science and Scripture*, (Grand Rapids: Eerdmans Publishing Co., 1954), pp. 296-298. G.C. Aalders, *The Problem of the Book of Jonah*, (London: Tyndale Press, 1948), p. 6. *Parade* magazine, (August 16, 1981).

22.   Harry Rimmer, *The Harmony of Science and Scripture*, (Grand Rapids: Eerdmans Publishing Co., 1936), Chapter 5.

23.   Harry Rimmer, *The Harmony of Science*

and Scripture, (Grand Rapids: Eerdmans Publishing Co., 1936), p. 184.

24. "When Animals Attack," (Sunday, April 28, 1996, 6 p.m., FOX, Channel 4).

25. "When the Sky Rained Fire," *Reader's Digest*, (February 1976).

26. Donald Patten and R. Hatch, *Joshua's Long Day and Six Other Catastrophes*, (Seattle, Washington: Pacific Meridian Publishing Co., 1973).

Bibliography

Archer, Gleason L. *Old Testament Introduction*.

Archer, Gleason L. *Encyclopedia of Bible Difficulties*. Michigan: The Zondervan Corp., 1982.

Berggren, W.A. and John A. Van Couvering. *Catastrophes and Earth History*. New Jersey: Princeton University Press, 1984.

Bourriau, Janine, Editor. *Understanding Catastrophe*. NY: Cambridge University Press, 1992.

Burl, Aubrey. *A Guide to the Stone Circles of Britain, Ireland and Brittany*. New Haven and London: Yale University, 1995.

Casson, Lionel. *Ancient Egypt*. Alexandria, VA: Time-Life Books,1965.

Erickson, Jon. *Target Earth!* Blue Ridge Summit, PA: TAB Books, 1991.

Funk and Wagnalls Standard Dictionary of Folklore Mythology and Legend, San Francisco, CA: Harper & Row, 1972.

Fox, Hugh. *Gods of the Cataclysm*, New York, NY: Dorset Press, 1981.

Gowlett, John. *Ascent to Civilization*, New York: Alfred A. Knopf Inc., 1984.

Grimal, Pierre. *Classical Mythology*, Massachusetts: Basil Blackwell Inc., 1986.

Graves, Robert and Raphael Patai. *Hebrew Myths, the Book of Genesis*. New York: Greenwich House, 1983.

Haley, John W. *Alleged Discrepancies of the Bible*, Michigan: Baker Book House, 1977.

Krupp, Dr. E.C. *Echoes of the Ancient Skies*, New York: Harper & Row, Publishers, 1983.

Leeming, David Adams. *The World of Myth*. New York Oxford: Oxford University Press, 1990.

Malek, Jaromir. *In the Shadow of the Pyramids*. Golden Press.

McKeever, Dr. James. *Believe It or Not ... It's in the Bible*. Oregon: Omega Publications, 1988.

Mercatante, Anthony S. *The Facts on File Encyclopedia of World Mythology and Legend*, United States of America: Library of Congress Cataloging in Publication Data, 1988.

Morris, Henry M. and Martin Clark. *The Bible Has the Answer*. San Diego, CA: Creation-Life Publishers Inc., 1976.

Neeve, David and K.O. Emery. *The Destruction of Sodom, Gomorrah and Jericho*. New York Oxford: Oxford University Press, 1995.

Patten, Donald R. Hatch. *The Long Day of Joshua and Six Other Catastrophes*. Seattle, WA: Pacific Meridian Publishing Co., 1973.

Patten, Donald W., *A Symposium on Creation*, Grand Rapids, MI: Baker Book House, 1975.

Rimmer, Harry. *The Harmony of Science and Scripture*. Grand Rapids, MI: Wm. B. Eerdmans Publishing Company, 1973.

Schaeffer, Edith. *Affliction*. Old Tappan, NJ: Fleming H. Revell Company, 1978.

Schaeffer, Francis A. *Joshua and the Flow of Biblical History*, Downers Grove, IL: InterVarsity Press, 1975.

Schilling, S. Paul. *God and Human Anguish*. Nashville, TN: Abingdon, 1977.

Stanton, Mary and Albert Hyma. *Streams of Civilization, Vol. One*. Arlington Heights, IL: Christian Liberty Press, 1992.

Time-Life Books. *Feats and Wisdom of the*

Ancients. Alexandria VA: Time-Life Books, 1990.

Time-Life Books. *Lost Civilizations Series, Aztecs: Reign of Blood & Splendor*. Alexandria VA: Time-Life Books Inc., 1992.

Time-Life Books, *Lost Civilizations Series, Pompeii: The Vanished City*. Alexandria, VA: Time-Life Books, 1992.

Time-Life Books. *Time-Frame Series, 3000-1500 BC, The Age of God-Kings*. Alexandria, Virginia: Time-Life Books, 1987.

Velikovsky, Immanuel, *Earth in Upheaval*, NY: Doubleday & Company Inc., 1968.

Velikovsky, Immanuel. *Worlds in Collision*. NY: Doubleday & Company Inc., 1950.

Watson, David C.C. *Myths & Miracles*. Worthing, Sussex: H.E. Walter Ltd., 1976.

Wenham, John W. *The Goodness of God*. Downers Grove, IL: InterVarsity Press, 1974.

Woodrow, Ralph Edward. *Noah's Flood, Joshua's Long Day, and Lucifer's Fall*. Riverside, CA: Ralph Woodrow Evangelistic Assoc. Inc., 1984.

Illustrations

1. The Missing Day 12
2. Science Versus Religion 20
3. A Pagan Conception 25
4. The Dance of the Universe 28
5. A Revolving Planet 32
6. Ancient I.D.s 34
7. The Ancient Seal 35
8. The Cylinder Seal 36
9. The Flat Earth Society 38
10. Texas Talk 47
11. Let the Whole World Rejoice 50
12. The Sunflower Came First 52
13. God's Great Rival. 54
14. The Disharmony of Creation and
    Evolutionism 58
15. God of War 68
16. Moral Depravity Among the
    Ancients 78
17. Moloch: A Gruesome God 81
18. Possessing the Land 84

19. Why the Walls Came
    Tumbling Down 88
20. An American Tragedy 98
21. An Abominable Custom 100
22. Temples of Death 103
23. Bloodthirsty Gods 104
24. Buried Alive: Pompeii,
    City of Death 110
25. Joshua and the Judge 123
26. Merry-Go-Round Factor 126
27. Plotting the Course 130
28. Tilt, Tilt, Tilt 132
29. The Earth's Angle 134
30. Seasonal Shifts 135
31. Arctic Circle 136
32. Midnight Sun 137
33. Planetary Tilts 138
34. Pointing Heavenward 143
35. Manipulating Magnetic Needles . . . 145
36. Invisible Forces 146
37. Earth's Magnetic Center 148
38. The Power of Magnets is Amazing . . 150
39. Earth's Magnetic Field 151
40. Earth's Magnetic Strength:
    Past and Future 154

41. Magnetic Beach Balls 156
42. Bizarre Beach Balls 158
43. A Miniature Magnetic Globe 161
44. Manipulating Magnetic Fields 162
45. Close Encounters of a
     Heavenly Kind 163
46. Simulating Joshua's Long Day 166
47. Tracking the Heavenly Visitor 169
48. Axis Shift 170
49. Hot Rock From Heaven 174
50. Heavenly Fallout 178
51. Asteroid Belt 181
52. Cataloging the Asteroids 183
53. Rochet's Limit 184
54. Rings and Plunging Missiles 185
55. Tektites: Liquid Blobs of Glass 187
56. Meteoroid Stream 189
57. The Great Siberian Explosion 191
58. The Tunguska Impact Area 193
59. Sodom and Gomorrah 194
60. An Ominous Omen in the Heavens . . 199
61. The Joshua Tree 203
62. Atlas of Legends 206
63. Monument to the Sun-God 211
64. Egyptian Temple of the Sun 213

65. Bird's-Eye View 214
66. Migration of the Sun 215
67. Ra, Ra, Ra for Ra 216
68. Stonehenge 219
69. The Wandering Sun 222
70. The Wobbling Earth 223
71. Toppling a Top 227
72. Wobbling Through the Heavens . . . 229
73. A Heavenly Encounter 230
74. Solar Eclipse 231
75. The Invisible Planet 233
76. Out of View, Out of Sight 234
77. The Obelisk: An Ancient Sundial . . 238
78. Tracking the Sun's Shadow 239
79. Reversing the Sun's Shadow 240
80. Satan's Temptation: "Did God ...?" . . 247
81. Jonah in the Whale 252
82. Giants of the Sea 258
83. Assigned to Assist Elijah 261
84. Swallowed by a Whale 262
85. The Assyrian Empire 271
86. Nineveh 272
87. Jonah's Trail 274
88. Missing God's Boat 276
89. About Face: Jonah's Footprints 280

90. Dagon, the Fish God 283
91. A Sign in the Heavens 286
92. Tracking the Heavenly Visitor 287
93. The Shroud 289
94. Chasing Rabbits 290
95. God Loves Children — and
     Animals Too 297
96. Gods of Cataclysm 306
97. Ascending to the Heavens 312
98. The Tower of Babel 317
99. The Towering Temples of Time . . . 318
100. Classical Gods of the Greeks 324
101. Mars Hill 330
102. Calendar Gods 333
103. Hallowed Night 335
104. Visitor for a Season 339
105. Demos and Phobos 341
106. Hairy Comet 343
107. Cataclysmic Tails 344
108. Doomsday Asteroid 354
109. Meteor Crater, Arizona 356
110. Cosmic Collision 359
111. Judgment Day for Planet Earth 360
112. The Fiery End 363
113. Target Earth 366

114. Destination Planet Earth 368
115. D-Day Planet Earth 371
116. Hellstorm 373
117. Cosmic Holocaust 374
118. Tongues of Fire 376
119. 9.8 Magnitude 377
120. 100-Pound Hailstones 378
121. Canteloupes Versus Watermelons . . 380
122. The Shepherd and His Sheep 382

Other Books in the
CREATION SCIENCE SERIES

by **Dennis Lindsay**